●= INTERVIEWING AND SELECTING HIGH PERFORMERS

A Practical Guide To Effective Hiring

Larry R. Smalley

Jossey-Bass
Pfeiffer
San Francisco

RICHARD
CHANG
ASSOCIATES

Published by

Jossey-Bass
Pfeiffer

350 Sansome Street, 5th Floor
San Francisco, California 94104-1342
(415) 433-1740; Fax (415) 433-0499
(800) 274-4434; Fax (800) 569-0443

www.pfeiffer.com

Printing   10   9   8   7   6   5   4   3   2   1

ACKNOWLEDGMENTS

About The Author

Larry Smalley, a Vice President and Principal Consultant for Richard Chang Associates, Inc., is a highly experienced, results-oriented human resources professional. His broad management background and demonstrated success in diverse environments allowed him to develop a proficiency in linking human resources systems to strategic business goals. He has particular expertise in organizational assessment and design, competency based selection and training systems, performance management implementation, compensation and incentive systems, and employee relations.

Larry would like to acknowledge the support of the entire team of professionals at Richard Chang Associates, Inc. for their contribution to the guidebook development process. In addition, special thanks are extended to the many client organizations who have helped us shape the practical ideas and proven methods shared in this guidebook.

Additional Credits

Editors: Ruth Stingley, Linda O'Key, and
                    Sarah Ortlieb Fraser

Reviewers: Rich Baisner, Shirley Codrey, Or Olvkovich,
                    and Susan Parker

Graphic Layout: Christina Slater

Cover Design: Eric Strand and John Odam Design Associates

PREFACE

The 1990's have already presented individuals and organizations with some very difficult challenges to face and overcome. So who will have the advantage as we move toward the year 2000 and beyond?

The advantage will belong to those with a commitment to continuous learning. Whether on an individual basis or as an entire organization, one key ingredient to building a continuous learning environment is *The Practical Guidebook Collection* brought to you by the Publications Division of Richard Chang Associates, Inc.

After understanding the future *"learning needs"* expressed by our clients and other potential customers, we are pleased to publish *The Practical Guidebook Collection*. These guidebooks are designed to provide you with proven, *"real-world"* tips, tools, and techniques—on a wide range of subjects—that you can apply in the workplace and/or on a personal level immediately.

Once you've had a chance to benefit from *The Practical Guidebook Collection*, please share your feedback with us. We've included a brief *Evaluation and Feedback Form* at the end of the guidebook that you can fax to us at (714) 727-7007.

With your feedback, we can continuously improve the resources we are providing through the Publications Division of Richard Chang Associates, Inc.

Wishing you successful reading,

Richard Y. Chang
President and CEO
Richard Chang Associates, Inc.

TABLE OF CONTENTS

"You're only as good as the people you hire."

Anonymous

CHAPTER ONE

INTRODUCTION

Why Read This Guidebook?

It's true. An organization is only as good as the people it employs. High-performing employees not only make your organization look good, they make the person who hired them look good. Face it: if you hire failures, both you and your organization will suffer. All top hiring managers know this and actively sharpen the skills it takes to interview and select high performers.

Now's your opportunity to learn what it takes to select the people who will make you and your organization shine. The high performers you select will not only fit their position descriptions, but also will be able to flex and multi-task when necessary.

Obviously, you won't be able to distinguish these select few from the crowd by using your *"gut instinct."* While this type of unstructured approach may pay off occasionally at the racetrack, who wants to take a gamble at work? Placing a bet on the wrong horse can cost you a few bucks, but that's nothing compared to the time and money your organization will waste if you hire the wrong person.

To avoid these stressful situations, you need to use a systematic selection process. *Interviewing And Selecting High Performers* will teach you that successful hiring is really about careful and accurate assessment and prediction. It will reveal the skills needed to assess past job performance and predict future success.

Who Should Read This Guidebook?

At some point in your management career, you'll be asked to hire someone. That isn't to say that this guidebook is for everyone. It's geared toward the needs of the hiring manager, supervisor, or team leader responsible for selecting and interviewing candidates.

Unless you hold a position in upper management or are a Human Resources professional, you probably will become the immediate supervisor of the person you hire. Your input is extremely valuable. After all, you should be well aware of the roles and responsibilities of the position, as well as the expertise and attitude needed in order for it to be performed successfully. A systematic interviewing and selecting process that will help you gauge these skills may prove to be a career-maker for you.

Commonly, organizations will ask an internal customer, supplier, or peer of the potential new-hire to interview the candidate. This multi-interviewer approach has been proven to increase the number of high performers hired. Give a copy of this guidebook to all of the interviewers involved in your interviewing and selecting process.

Whether you are responsible for the entire process or just a part of it, use *Interviewing And Selecting High Performers* as your guide to picking the best people out of the sea of resumes and getting them on board at your organization.

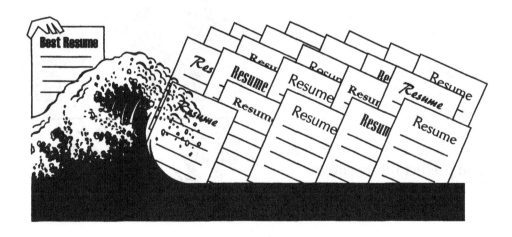

When And How To Use It

Interviewing And Selecting High Performers describes a process that works best if adopted throughout your organization. However, your organization may already have some sort of hiring process, or maybe they have no process in place at all. It doesn't matter. You still need to interview, and you're still responsible for the people you hire. Read this guidebook and watch as your efforts are rewarded.

If you chose this guidebook because you're interested in improving performance in your organization, you made a good choice. Additionally, consider reading the other guidebooks published by Richard Chang Associates, Inc. that deal with the Performance Management Cycle. Once you've hired top performers, you need to plan for their performance, coach them, and successfully evaluate them.

Whatever your situation, the performance-based process in this guidebook will pay off as soon as you begin to use it. *(One "good hire" will more than reimburse you for the investment of your time.)* Presumably, you've been asked to hire someone. If this is your first hiring experience, read this entire guidebook before you begin. You will be completing worksheets that will become tools to guide you throughout the interviewing and selecting process.

If you've hired dozens of employees, you're probably looking to increase your success rate. Read this guidebook selectively, taking note of the tips and adding elements to your pre-existing process. And, if your hiring results have been disastrous or even so-so, don't delay. Read *Interviewing And Selecting High Performers* as soon as possible. It will help set you on the path to making the right choices.

Whatever the case, you need to read this guidebook before you even begin screening applicants. Do it now.

THE BIG PICTURE

Performance-Based Interviewing And Selecting Is Crucial

You already know that acquiring good people is a *"must"* for your organization. Hiring an outstanding employee is a prime opportunity to demonstrate your good sense and judgment. Don't blow it! Use performance-based interviewing and selecting to rout out the most important information about a prospective employee's past behavior.

"Why focus on past behavior?" you may ask. Because, if applicants were successful in their past jobs, they're more likely to be successful in your organization. In the chapters that follow, you'll learn to use carefully phrased questions to uncover a candidate's past behavior. And, once you know what type of behavior you can expect from a potential employee, you'll be able to determine that person's fit within your organization.

Many managers don't know how to do this. Even those with years of interviewing experience report that they wind up talking about 75 percent of the time during interviews. If you end up dominating the conversation, your candidate won't have the time to share what you need to know about him or her.

The fact is, most types of interviewing don't allow you to get down to the *"real"* business of the interview—uncovering information about the candidate. The best interviews are those in which the interviewer steps back and gently guides the flow of information. Your goal is to control the interview by keeping your talk to a minimum, all the while encouraging your candidate to respond to performance-based questions.

Choosing the right questions to ask when you interview your candidates is critical. And, in some cases, the questions you ask may have legal limitations. For example, over the last two decades, beginning with the passage of the Civil Rights Act of 1964, the United States government has played an ever-increasing role in saying what employers can and cannot do in the course of the selection process.

Specifically, employers are cautioned against asking certain kinds of questions which, either directly or by inference, violate the law in its word or meaning. Being conscious to only ask *"job-related"* questions is a key guideline to help you avoid illegal problems. You should always avoid questions concerning age, race, color, national origin, religion, physical handicap, marital status, or sex, which might be interpreted as being in violation of any laws.

Make it a point to learn what's acceptable or not. If you have any concerns about questions you'd like to ask, always check with your organization's Human Resources or legal department.

Choosing The Best Type Of Interviewing

What type of interview will bring out the information you need? It depends. Take a moment to review the four basic types, and you'll be able to identify what will work for you.

Structured interviewing

Structured interviewing is acceptable if you are looking for someone to fill a highly-structured position requiring specific skills *(e.g., payroll clerk)*. In a structured interview, you ask the same set of questions you've asked your other candidates, and you record responses word-for-word.

Open-Ended Interviewing

"Tell me about yourself..."

Open-ended interviewing allows candidates the opportunity to talk about their work, life, and goals. Trained professionals tend to use this approach when conducting executive assessments, but the average interviewer usually has a difficult time sorting valuable data from general information.

Stress/Pressure Interviewing

"Why do you think you are qualified for the job? Go ahead—sell me right now!"

Stress/pressure interviewing is rarely an interviewer's first choice, but is sometimes acceptable when a position requires candidates to withstand great stress. In stress/pressure interviewing, candidates are challenged to react quickly to *"fake"* pressure. For example, an interviewer might demand a candidate to answer a pointed question within five seconds.

Performance-Based Interviewing

Performance-based interviewing probes for the *"how"* and the *"what,"* not the philosophical *"why."* Performance-based interviewing is an ideal choice when dealing with candidates for virtually any type of job. This type of interviewing not only covers technical aspects of a position, but it also zeroes in on past behavior which tells you how candidates will fit in your organization.

If You're Still Not Convinced...

"How do you organize your workday?"

Check it out for yourself. Study the following pros and cons of each interviewing type, and you'll soon decide that performance-based interviewing is the best choice for most situations.

STRUCTURED INTERVIEWING

Pros:
- Valid method of comparison
- Reliable
- Provides even playing field

Cons:
- Difficult to assess subtle qualities
- Superficial
- Can produce false negatives (*i.e., can result in rejection of well-qualified candidates*)
- Monotonous for both interviewer and candidate

OPEN-ENDED INTERVIEWING

Pros:
- Provides more rounded view of candidate
- Reveals candidate's values and interests

Cons:
- May gloss over technical skills and behavior
- May provide more philosophy than fact
- Often lengthy and rambling
- Difficult to interpret and compare
- May over-emphasize candidate's likability

STRESS/PRESSURE INTERVIEWING

Pros:
- Adequately screens candidates

Cons:
- Provokes abnormal candidate behavior
- Produces many false negatives
- Doesn't adequately predict future performance

PERFORMANCE-BASED INTERVIEWING

Pros:

- Produces data which reveals previous behavior
- Is relatively easy to interpret and compare
- Provides insight into future job performance
- Probes for specific facts, not philosophy
- Gets candidate to be candid and open with interviewer

Cons:

- May require effort to keep candidate on track
- If past position is not similar to position desired, may be difficult to gauge

Pretty clear, isn't it? Performance-based interviewing does have a couple of drawbacks, but they are certainly surmountable. When you make the effort to understand and use performance-based interviewing, you'll learn to overcome most obstacles to emerge with a winner.

The Performance-Based Selection Process

You can read all you want to about the benefits of performance-based interviewing, but unless you know what to do, you'll still be wondering how to hire a *"star"* candidate. The Performance-Based Selection Process presented in this guidebook will provide you with the means to interview and select high performers. Its five easy-to-follow steps will keep you on track.

Step 5: Offering

Step 4: Selecting

Step 3: Interviewing

Step 2: Screening

Step 1: Preparing

Quickly scan the steps of the process above. You'll immediately notice that *"interviewing"* appears in the center. There's a good reason for this. Successful interviews don't begin when a candidate walks into your office; they begin with adequate *"preparation."*

Many people think of *"preparation"* as a negative. Why? Because it takes work. But no one ever argued that people who prepare extensively for an event—such as a trade show—don't end up ahead of those who don't. Likewise, you must prepare up-front for your interviews. If you don't, you'll end up working twice as hard just to make it through the selection process with no guarantee of success.

However, if you approach the actual interview adequately prepared, the rest of the process will be easy. You'll find the work is worth it. So stop wasting time thinking of excuses as to why you don't have time to prepare. In order for this process to work, you're going to have to prepare and organize up-front.

The next step in the Performance-Based Selection Process will help you to drastically narrow the scope of your search. You will build on your preparation by *screening* your applicants, determining the few who will go on to be interviewed. If you're having trouble finding candidates, refer to the *"Recruiting Checklist"* in the Appendix for some ideas.

Then, when you get to the *interviewing* step, you will again refine your search, using proven techniques that will yield the best results.

Your post-interview steps are just as important. In *selecting* the final candidate, you will assess any important technical skills, and you'll compare notes with all those who interviewed the candidates. You'll zero in on the best fit among your final candidates.

And in the final step, *offering*, you'll learn how to formally and officially get your best candidate on board. This may seem straightforward, but sometimes this is the stage of the game where your best candidates might *"fall through the cracks."* You don't want that to happen.

Even if the responsibility for hiring is in your hands, you'll be enlisting the help of your peers, Human Resources people, and others within your organization to independently confirm and validate your choices. And if you are the Human Resources professional responsible for hiring, you too should use others to help you select the best candidate. While the extent of others' involvement in the process is your decision, their input will increase the probability of a successful hire.

Within this guidebook, a complete chapter is devoted to each step of the Performance-Based Selection Process. Take a look at what's involved in each of the five steps.

Step 1: Preparing

- Complete a Position Requirements Worksheet
- Design performance-based questions
- Determine how to evaluate technical skills

Step 2: Screening

- Screen resumes by using an A-B-C rating system
- Conduct phone screening
- Set up interviews

Step 3: Interviewing

- Gather job-related data
- Provide information
- Discuss what happens next and wrap up

Step 4: Selecting

- ◆ Conduct non-interviewing assessment of technical skills
- ◆ Complete the Candidate Comparison Sheet
- ◆ Conduct reference checks on final top candidates

Step 5: Offering

- ◆ Determine offer components
- ◆ Make a verbal and a written offer
- ◆ Inform non-selected candidates of your decision

Now that you've got the big picture, it's time to look at the specifics. Read each section of this guidebook carefully, and put some thought into the worksheet exercises. In many cases, these exercises will evolve into the actual tools you will be using during each step.

The Performance-Based Selection Process, which uses multiple interviewers, will result in increased selection quality. You owe it to yourself and your organization to get busy and learn what it takes to make this process work for you. To help you through it, you'll be given the opportunity to see how an individual in one organization takes on the task of hiring her replacement. Read on.

Welcome to Mother Earth, Inc.,...
an expanding organization, founded eight years ago as a manufacturer of earth-friendly household cleaning products and detergents. Initially founded to appeal to a niche market, Mother Earth has survived the vogue status of the green movement, and now appeals to a wider range of consumers.

A guiding force behind this success has been innovative advertising and marketing strategies. Highlighting everything from the products' low phosphorous content to the reusable packaging, these ad campaigns have been gradually expanding into more and varied types of media. The marketing department recently launched an in-store comparison campaign that has already boosted sales.

Mother Earth, Inc. purposely carries its conscientious approach over into its hiring practices as well. The company offers employees ownership and innovative benefits packages, and it consistently promotes from within.

Anika Jordan is moving up in the organization. She came aboard four years ago as the receptionist for the Marketing Department at the Mother Earth, Inc. headquarters in the Northwest. Now, one of her supervisors has been promoted, leaving Anika free to step up to the position of Marketing Coordinator, a position which specializes in the organization's set-ups at trade shows.

Anika's task is to hire a new receptionist for the twenty-person Marketing Department, so she can move into her new position. Although Anika felt her boss did a fairly decent job of hiring her, she thought the process could be improved upon. She asked for advice, and was led to a manager who shared the Performance-Based Selection Process with her. At image-conscious Mother Earth, Inc., Anika knows that the receptionist is a highly-visible, important position. The organization is willing to pay more than the average salary in order to gain a valuable employee. Anika wants to find the right one.

Anika knows she has her work cut out for her, but she's willing to tackle it. After all, if she hires a great receptionist, it'll make her position easier to handle.

CHAPTER TWO WORKSHEET:
WHAT'S WRONG WITH INTERVIEWING?

In any interviewing and selecting process, certain problems may prevent you from hiring the best candidate. Listed below are some common problems. Review each; then list the impact of each problem and your ideas for overcoming it.

THE DEADLY SEVEN INTERVIEWING PROBLEMS

1. Problem: Unclear, ambiguous position requirements

Impact of problem:

_____

_____

Ways to overcome:

_____

_____

2. Problem: Selection criteria not well-defined or not communicated

Impact of problem:

_____

_____

Ways to overcome:

_____

_____

INTERVIEWING AND SELECTING HIGH PERFORMERS   15

3. Problem: Improper interviewing type

Impact of problem:

_____

_____

Ways to overcome:

_____

_____

4. Problem: *"Warm body" syndrome (i.e., low standards, resulting in the selection of mediocre people)*

Impact of problem:

_____

_____

Ways to overcome:

_____

_____

5. Problem: Interviewer dominates the interview

Impact of problem:

_____

_____

Ways to overcome:

_____

_____

6. | Problem: Questions do not focus on past behavior or technical skills |

Impact of problem:

_____

_____

Ways to overcome:

_____

_____

7. | Problem: Improper screening techniques *(e.g., rejecting applicants from Ivy League schools due to personal bias)* |

Impact of problem:

_____

_____

Ways to overcome:

_____

_____

PREPARING FOR SUCCESS
IN THE INTERVIEW

 It isn't glamorous. It's seldom fun. And, oftentimes, it's downright tedious. However, you must do it. You must adequately prepare if you want to hire a high performer.

Who prepared the supplies the last time you went camping, sailing, or even picnicking? If you forgot something important, you probably had to alter your plans or *"make do"* with something else. You don't want that to happen when the hiring of a new employee is at stake. A lack of planning in the interviewing and selecting process can have a negative impact on the future of your organization.

Overview Of The "Preparing" Step

Effective preparation will help you set the stage for a great interview. This step involves:

☑ Completing a Position Requirements Worksheet that will help you *screen* applicants prior to the interview,

☑ Designing performance-based questions that will help you *assess* candidates during the interviews, and

☑ Determining the best method for evaluating technical skills that will help you *select* the best candidate after the interviews.

In this preparation step, you'll be focusing in on the requirements of the position and the type of person who'd be the best match for it. To do this, you first have to identify the open position's functions and responsibilities.

Ask yourself:

> "What will the person we hire be responsible for (i.e., what will he or she have to do to be successful in this position)?"

Answering this question will open the door to helping you figure out the requirements for the position. You'll need to answer it, because you can't complete the preparation step until you do. Coming up with the functions and responsibilities of the position enables you both to complete the Position Requirements Worksheet and to design your performance-based interview questions.

The requirements you will determine after you have identified the functions and responsibilities fall into three major categories:

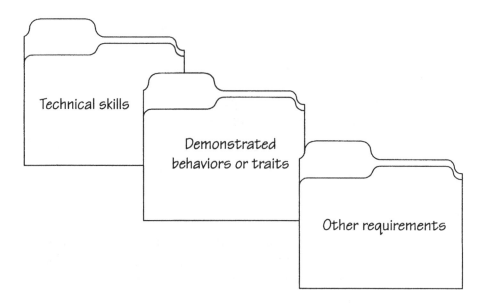

Technical skills

Demonstrated behaviors or traits

Other requirements

Technical skills

These are any required technical skills that the person you hire must have mastered. For example, if a function of the new X-ray technician you want to hire is to perform ultrasound exams, you may demand that she can successfully use the specific ultrasound equipment you recently purchased. You'll be listing technical skills on the Position Requirements Worksheet.

Demonstrated behaviors or traits

Demonstrated behaviors or traits refer to the types of behavior and/or the kinds of traits you're looking for in the person you hire. For example, based on the functions and responsibilities of the open position, you may determine that you want someone with intellectual curiosity or you need a person with superb organizational skills.

You'll be focusing a great deal of time and energy on this category. Why? It's not that difficult to evaluate technical skills or to determine other requirements (*e.g., a glance at a resume can tell you about the educational background of an applicant, and a typing test can tell you how many words per minute a candidate can type*). However, behaviors and traits aren't so obvious, and yet they are a great indicator of performance on the job. The way you determine them is through asking performance-based questions during your interview. You will be designing your questions based on the behaviors and traits you've listed for the open position.

Other requirements

This category contains any requirements that don't fit in the other two categories. Examples include values, education, location, travel, and compensation. If you need to hire a public relations person, you may require a bachelor's degree in a related field, and you may determine that your salary limit for the position is $30,000. You'll be listing these other requirements on your Position Requirements Worksheet.

Addressing each of these three categories will put you ahead of the game in this preparation step. You'll know exactly what you want in a candidate, and you'll know what to ask to determine if a particular candidate has what it takes. You're on the road to making your work life easier.

Complete A Position Requirements Worksheet

A Position Requirements Worksheet provides you with a snapshot of the open position. The more complete and in focus the picture is, the easier it will be for you to match the person who will fit the description. The investment of time in this worksheet will pay big dividends later.

If your organization requires that you fill out a personnel requisition, you can use it in addition to or instead of filling out the Position Requirements Worksheet that follows. *(You'll find a copy of a blank Position Requirements Worksheet in the Appendix.)* Either way, you need to know the following information if you want your interviews to be productive:

1. The title of the open position, the date it opens, and your need for the position. In other words, if you're hiring a sales representative, you'd list that title, the date when you need the position filled, and why you need it filled (e.g., *upper management has added another sales territory to your region, and you need someone to handle the new territory by the beginning of next month*). This may sound simple, but doing it clarifies for all interviewers the basic information related to the position. When you're finished with the preparation step, you'll know what to screen for.

2. The functions and responsibilities of the open position. If you have already determined these, list them. If not, brainstorm possible ideas by yourself or with others in your organization. The job description (*if available*) will be a big help.

3. The technical skills you require from the person who will fill the position.

4. Other requirements you expect from your applicants.

Keep the following criteria in mind as you pick your selection requirements. They should be...

1. **Specific In Nature**—Word each requirement precisely (*e.g., make one of your requirements "Analytical Reasoning" instead of "Intelligence"*).

2. **Appropriate In Number**—Keep the number of your requirements in the 3-15 range (*if you have too few, you may not screen out poor applicants; too many, and you may end up with no candidates to interview*).

4. **Applied Consistently**—Finally, limit your requirements to those that will be applied to every candidate. Any with overt or implied bias should be discarded (*e.g., you would not have a requirement that states, "If a female, must not be pregnant"*).

Back at Mother Earth, Inc.,...

Anika decided to fill out a Position Requirements Worksheet before she screened the receptionist applicants. She asked Marion Bliesmer, the executive assistant for the company CEO, and Greg Chandler, manager of the Marketing Department, to help her. Together, the three brainstormed the requirements and came up with the following:

POSITION REQUIREMENTS WORKSHEET

Title: Receptionist/Marketing Department   **Date Open:** March 3, XXXX
Need For Position: Anika Jordan has been promoted to Marketing Coordinator

FUNCTIONS AND RESPONSIBILITIES

I. Interface with visitors:
   A. Greet them courteously
   B. Question them politely
   C. Direct them efficiently

II. Manage the phone system:
   A. Answer incoming calls
   B. Program and modify voice-mail system when necessary
   C. Screen callers and take messages as required

III. Provide administrative support:
   A. Formulate memos, proposals, and requisitions for the Marketing Department
   B. Address and meter envelopes
   C. Handle administrative overflow when necessary

TECHNICAL SKILLS

Word processing skills, ability to operate postage meter and overnight mail tracking software, ability to operate and program voice-mail systems.

OTHER REQUIREMENTS

◆ Bachelor's degree preferred

◆ Desire to move up within the company a plus

◆ Early start time required (e.g. 7 a.m., M-F)

◆ Availability for relocation within 2-3 years, due to projected change in corporate headquarters

Design Performance-Based Questions

At this point, you will design questions based on the same functions and responsibilities you identified on the Position Requirements Worksheet. To help you design effective performance-based questions, you can use the Performance-Based Interview Questions Worksheet that follows. If you filled out a Position Requirements Worksheet, transfer the functions and responsibilities from that worksheet onto the Performance-Based Interview Questions Worksheet. *(See the Appendix for a blank copy of this worksheet also.)*

Working from your list of functions and responsibilities, identify the traits required to handle those responsibilities. You will find that some functions and responsibilities require several demonstrated behavioral traits, while others require only one. *(See the Appendix for a list of demonstrated behaviors or traits and related questions.)*

Don't worry about testing technical skills or questioning candidates on other requirements at this point. Remember, most problems on the job are related to *"behavior,"* not the inability to fulfill technical requirements. Yes, you will also develop questions about technical expertise; however, technical expertise is often tested in other ways. Right now, your goal is to come up with a set of questions that will be used to assess behaviors and traits.

At Mother Earth, Inc.,...

Anika also asked Marion and Greg for their input on the Performance-Based Interview Questions Worksheet. The first part was simple; they just transferred the functions and responsibilities identified on their Position Requirements Worksheet. Together, then, they came up with the behaviors and traits listed on the following page.

OPEN POSITION: Receptionist/Marketing Department	
FUNCTIONS AND RESPONSIBILITIES	**DEMONSTRATED BEHAVIORS OR TRAITS**
I. Interface with visitors	
A. Greet them courteously **B.** Question them politely **C.** Direct them efficiently	**1.** Professional bearing **2.** Communication skills **3.** Enthusiasm for customer service
II. Manage the phone system	
A. Answer incoming calls **B.** Program and modify voice-mail system, when necessary **C.** Screen callers and take messages, as required	**1.** Initiative **2.** Judgment **3.** Detail-orientation
III. Provide administrative support	
A. Formulate memos, proposals, and requisitions for the Marketing Department **B.** Address and meter envelopes **C.** Handle administrative overflow, when necessary	**1.** Teamwork **2.** Flexibility

Anika, Marion, and Greg made an effort not to duplicate any behaviors or traits, and they looked at each to see which was the best fit. Then they began to think in terms of questions that would uncover each identified behavior or trait.

Some of these demonstrated behaviors or traits would be difficult to evaluate by asking a single question, such as: *"Are you detail-oriented?"* or *"Do you act in a professional manner?"* Their questions would have to uncover *how* each candidate performed or behaved in past positions. They'd have to come up with some really good questions....

What's A Good Question?

A good interview starts with really good questions. Think about the types of questions you think might help to uncover the behaviors or traits you have identified on the Performance-Based Interview Questions Worksheet. Before you create them, however, consider the following guidelines:

MAXIMIZE QUESTIONS THAT ARE:	MINIMIZE QUESTIONS THAT ARE:	COMPLETELY AVOID QUESTIONS THAT ARE:
• Job-related • Focused on past behavior • Open-ended	• Directed • Hypothetical • Easily answered with a *"yes"* or *"no"*	• Discriminatory • Leading • Trick/ psychological

If these guidelines disqualify most of the questions you have begun to develop, don't despair. You can easily upgrade a question through careful rephrasing. *(Refer to "What's A Good Question?" in the Appendix. In addition, you can choose questions directly from the list of "Performance-Based Interview Questions," also in the Appendix. Why reinvent the wheel?!)*

For instance, begin your questions with words or phrases like *"Tell me about"* or *"How."* They encourage a detailed response by asking for a description or by inviting comparison between two subjects. Also encourage the candidate to categorize his or her own performance by asking a question such as, *"How was your selling record at your last organization?"* Leading questions, such as, *"Was your selling record up to par?"* should be avoided.

In addition, stick to the facts by asking how things *have* been done in the past. Avoid inviting hypothetical responses by asking candidates how *would* they handle something.

Occasionally, you may have to use a direct question to find out if a prospective employee's opinion is in line with yours or that of your organization. In this case, asking the question *"Did you find...?"* is acceptable, but may put the candidate on the defensive and break down rapport as a result. Aim to limit the number of direct-response questions on your list. Instead, try to get the information in another way.

Remember, most people like talking about themselves. Your goal is to try to get them to expand on a specific topic. Choose questions that are respectful in tone and content; don't try to catch candidates off-guard or *"trick"* them into revealing information. The candidate in your office today may be a future customer or may be interviewing *you* at some point down the line!

At Mother Earth, Inc.,...

Anika, Marion, and Greg bounced questions off of each other, and came up with a good list. They took each behavior or trait listed in the middle column of the Performance-Based Interview Questions Worksheet and wrote a couple of possible questions to gauge each trait.

DEMONSTRATED BEHAVIORS OR TRAITS	PERFORMANCE-BASED INTERVIEW QUESTIONS
I. A. 1. Professional bearing	1. How did you handle that very persistent walk-in salesperson at your last position? 2. How did you deal with confidential or discretionary information?
I.B. 2. Communication skills	3. What is it about yourself that makes you effective when speaking to people? 4. What difficulties have you encountered communicating with others?

DEMONSTRATED BEHAVIORS OR TRAITS	PERFORMANCE-BASED INTERVIEW QUESTIONS
I.C.3. Enthusiasm for customer service	5. Tell me about a typical customer service problem at your last organization. 6. How did you handle it?
II.A.1. Initiative	7. What new procedures or improvements did you bring to your last job? 8. How have you assisted others in your work? 9. What have you done when you've been confronted by a problem that seemed to demand your manager's attention, and your manager was not available?
II.B.2. Judgment	10. What was your reason for leaving your last job? 11. How did you maintain accuracy during periods of frequent interruptions?
II.C.3. Detail-orientation	12. What did you do when your work was returned to you for correction?
III.A.1. Teamwork	13. What behaviors have made you an effective team member? 14. How have you responded to feedback from other team members regarding your performance?
III.B.2. Flexibility	15. What do you normally do when your routine is disrupted? 16. How many hours per week have you devoted to your job?

As they went along, Anika, Marion, and Greg imagined the range of responses each question could elicit and how they would react to each. If their reaction was decisive, they decided that the question was a *"keeper."*

Now that the behavioral assessment was in place, Anika's next task was to decide how to efficiently measure the technical requirements of the position....

Determine How To Evaluate Technical Skills

The performance-based questions you have designed will address the behavioral aspects of the position you are seeking to fill. However, the successful candidate for the position will not only possess the desired behaviors or traits, but also will have mastered all of the required technical skills.

The last task in the preparation step is to decide how to measure these technical skills. Options include:

1. Interview by expert
2. Testing
3. In-basket assessment

If you will be the immediate supervisor of the person you will hire, you know how to question the candidate about necessary technical skills. At other times, however, you may seek an expert interviewer. An expert interviewer not only can provide you with an assessment of the candidate's technical skills, but he or she can also give you an independent evaluation of the candidate's suitability for the position.

The second option, testing, provides an opportunity for objective measurement. Typing tests were the norm for most clerical positions of years past; now, however, word-processing tests are routinely given by most employers. Many positions that require written reports, such as insurance estimator, require basic grammar and spelling tests. And some tests, such as welding tests, are required by law or by hiring custom.

Some positions don't lend themselves well to traditional testing methods. In these cases, a particularly innovative method—called an *"in-basket assessment"*—can be used. This works particularly well for positions as diverse as a purchasing manager for a retail firm or even a traffic manager for a radio station.

The assessment works like this: the candidate is given a specific time period in which to go through the contents of a typical in-basket filled with sample documents. The candidate is asked to route, classify, and prioritize these documents, perhaps coming up with a schedule or roster as a result.

Before you decide on the method of evaluating technical skills, ask yourself the following questions:

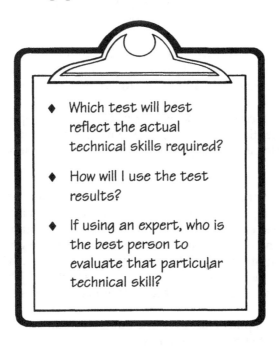

♦ Which test will best reflect the actual technical skills required?

♦ How will I use the test results?

♦ If using an expert, who is the best person to evaluate that particular technical skill?

Evaluating technical skills is usually a straightforward task and does not require as much thought as preparing performance-based questions. However, it is important, because it often determines whether or not a candidate is qualified. Your main objective is to make sure the evaluation method is realistic and fair.

At Mother Earth, Inc.,…

Anika researched the evaluation methods available to her and decided on two that would cover the technical aspects of the receptionist position.

First, she decided to submit all candidates to a test on the word-processing program currently used at Mother Earth. She would have applicants type handwritten notes into a marketing requisition, as well as formulate a memorandum using a sample of the format used by the organization.

Anika also planned to have Carl Trang, *"the phone guru,"* conduct a test of the candidates' skills in using the phone system. Together, they designed a test that first would quickly show each candidate how to transfer, hold, and send calls into the voice-mail system. Then, the candidates would be asked to field sample calls and be graded on the efficiency of their performance. Anika also asked Carl to observe the perceived pleasantness of each candidate's phone voice and demeanor. He would assign a *"pass"* or *"fail"* to these aspects of the candidate's performance.

At one point, Anika considered having each candidate track a sample package on the overnight-mail tracking system, but discarded that notion, deciding finally that she did not want to overwhelm the candidates.

Unbelievably *(it seemed)*, Anika was finished with her preparation work. She felt it was rather tiresome at first, but the more she put into it, the more confident she felt about the process. In fact, she was beginning to review resumes.

Some resumes came from the walk-in traffic Anika dealt with as receptionist for the Marketing Department. She retained the names and numbers of anyone who had expressed interest in an entry-level position at the organization and contacted this group of people, soliciting resumes from those who were still interested. In addition, she contacted a couple of reliable employment agencies in the area, ran an internal job posting through the organization's e-mail, and placed ads in the *Seattle Post*.

Anika now had a pile of just over one-hundred resumes. From those resumes, she had to find the *"perfect fit."*

Your preparation is done! If you have handled it well, the rest of the process will definitely be easier. Get ready to sift through that pile of resumes and distinguish those candidates you will be meeting in face-to-face interviews. You will learn the ins and outs of screening in the next chapter.

CHAPTER THREE WORKSHEET:
MASTERING THE PREPARING STEP

1. Look at the function and responsibilities listed below for the position of Consumer Affairs Specialist. Identify up to three demonstrated behaviors or traits for each responsibility.

OPEN POSITION: Consumer Affairs Specialist	
FUNCTIONS AND RESPONSIBILITIES	DEMONSTRATED BEHAVIORS OR TRAITS
I. Handle incoming customer phone calls	
A. Identify need of customer	1. 2. 3.
B. Develop options to resolve problems	1. 2. 3.
C. Close call with a commitment	1. 2. 3.

2. Now, on another sheet of paper, devise two questions that relate to each demonstrated behavior or trait. (*If you prefer, you may use a blank Performance-Based Interview Question Worksheet, inserting the functions and responsibilities for a position you currently have available at your organization.*) Review "*Performance-Based Interview Questions*" in the Appendix for possible questions that you can use.

SCREENING YOUR APPLICANTS

 Your preparation is behind you. You are finally ready to begin looking at potential employees on paper to see how they size up. Should you just start plowing through resumes? Hardly. Effective screening is just as important as careful preparation.

Screening is both a time- and a money-saver. Interviewing certainly takes time. So why waste your time *(and money, since time is money)*, as well as your applicants', by setting up interviews that prove to be unsuccessful within the first few minutes? Proper screening will help ensure that the candidate sitting in front of you during an interview is at least somewhere in the ballpark, if not *the* player you want on your team.

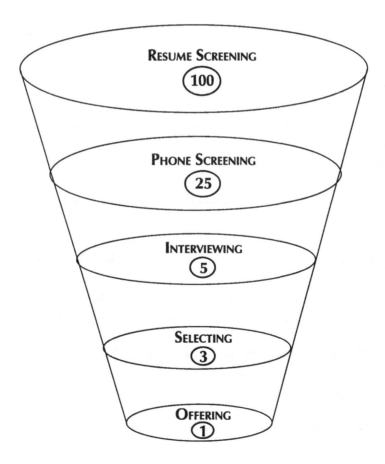

In this screening step, you'll be:

☑ Screening the resumes from your applicant pool,

☑ Conducting effective phone screening of your chosen applicants, and

☑ Setting up your interviews.

Screen The Resumes From Your Applicant Pool

As a manager, you probably already have a system in place to help you prioritize your goals, objectives, and even the events that make up your daily schedule. Most likely, you prioritize items within these groups according to their importance.

If so, screening resumes should come naturally to you. Begin by sifting through the resumes you've received from applicants interested in the position you have open. Then rank each of them. You'll use the Position Requirements Worksheet you filled out in Chapter Two to rank the resumes according to the number of requirements they meet. You should end up with three stacks of resumes, as follows:

"A" RESUMES: Resumes that appear to fulfill *all or most* of requirements listed on your Position Requirements Worksheet.

"B" RESUMES: Resumes that appear to fulfill *some* of the requirements listed on your Position Requirements Worksheet.

"C" RESUMES: Resumes that appear to fulfill *few or none* of the requirements listed on your Position Requirements Worksheet.

Rank each resume fairly and consistently. If all the resumes end up in the B or C group, you're either grading too hard, or you need to generate more applicants. If most of the resumes end up in the A pile, your requirements may need to be more specific.

This step of the process may cause you to feel a little stressed, or even to question your own good judgment. Never fear: remember, you will be using a multi-interviewer approach. This applies to all of the steps in the Performance-Based Selection Process. So call in an additional person to help with the screening of your applicants.

Obviously, you should seek help from someone who has good judgment and is familiar with the position you are seeking to fill. However, if you feel you may have been too generous with the applicants, choose someone that you perceive to be *"tougher"* than yourself. Conversely, if you feel you may have been excessively harsh, choose someone more tolerant; his or her judgment will complement yours.

Show your helper the Position Requirements Worksheet and the stack of A and B resumes, and review each of them along with him. Have him further refine and revise the content of these two groups, relegating some to the C stack, if necessary.

At this point, you should strive to keep the resumes in your combined A and B groups to a manageable number *(around twenty to twenty-five)*. If you keep more than that, you will be spending too much time on the phone screening applicants.

Conduct Effective Phone Screening Of Your Chosen Applicants

While phone screening will help to narrow the focus of your candidate search, it does not take the place of a face-to-face interview. Keep in mind that about 60 percent of any communicated message is lost when the nonverbal portion is removed.

Phone screening is not the time to dip into your arsenal of performance-based interview questions. Rather, use phone screening to clarify the contents of the resume or weed out applicants on the basis of salary requirements, working hours, or relocation issues. It provides an ideal opportunity to question the applicants about any requirements in the categories of *"technical skills"* or *"other requirements"* that you listed on the Position Requirements Worksheet.

Before you start your phone screens, however, you'll have to determine who is your best choice to conduct phone screening. You may choose from among those who will be assisting you in actually interviewing the candidates, or you may choose to use people from your support staff. Or, your organization may have specific members of the Human Resources staff who perform this function.

Don't spend too much time agonizing over these choices. Each screener will be working from a *"script"* consisting of a list of questions, and will be recording responses as the screening progresses. If you wish, you may choose to use the Phone Screen Organizer found in the Appendix. On it, you can list the questions you want your screeners to ask.

In addition to determining who will screen your applicants, determine when. It is probably appropriate to give your screeners a specific time period in which to conduct their phone screens. Get a firm commitment on this. Any delays may result in your top candidates being snapped up by your organization's competitors!

Make sure that both you and your additional phone screeners are aware of how to conduct effective phone screens. Consider the following:

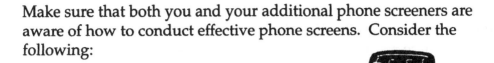

1. Review the resumes from your A and B applicant groups.

2. Create a list of questions to ask based upon *"other requirements"* and *"technical skills." (Do not make notations on the resume itself. Writing on original resumes could cause legal difficulties down the line.)*

3. Give the questions to your designated phone screener(s) *(including yourself). (If this is your first time through the Performance-Based Selection Process, you may choose to screen some applicants personally; it will help you "get your feet wet.")*

4. When you call, be sensitive to the needs of the applicants. Be sure to contact applicants at home unless specific consent has been given to contact them at their current place of employment. Also, determine if the applicants have sufficient time to go through the questions *(most phone screens will last fifteen to thirty minutes).*

5. Allow for flexibility if applicants are unavailable *(e.g., schedule the call for after-hours or over the weekend if an applicant is not available during working hours.)*

6. Ask candidates each question, and take detailed notes of each response *(on a separate sheet).* Focus on the words, not the tone *(i.e., substance over style).* After all, some people who may not be very conversational on the phone still make excellent employees. Also, as necessary, ask applicants to clarify their resumes.

7. Keep the conversation moving and allow applicants to talk about 80 percent of the time.

8. Fill the prospective candidates in on the next step in the process. Concentrate on the positive aspects, informing the applicants that, if selected, they will receive a call to schedule an interview. Hold off on deciding exactly who you will be interviewing until you have compared the results of each phone screen. Remain open. Do not get *"married"* to any one applicant.

When you have the results of your phone screens in your hands, go through them carefully. You should be able to toss out many on the basis of these results; the rest are likely to be good choices for face-to-face interviews. Hold on to the best of these *(approximately five or six, if you started with an adequate number of resumes)*. You're nearly ready for interviewing. The rejected applicants from the A and B groups *(and all applicants in the C group)* will be notified later in the process that they are no longer being considered.

Set Up Your Interviews

A piece of the *"how"* of interviewing is the *"who"* (i.e., *Who will conduct the interviews?*). The multi-interviewer approach is still the best choice for hiring winners. However, unlike phone screening, where you split up the applicants among interviewers, face-to-face interviewing requires each interviewer to question each candidate.

In general, your interviewers should be future peers, customers of, or suppliers to the position. For example, a member of the work group that puts together the organization's newsletter would be a good choice for an interviewer of your candidates for a desktop-publisher position.

Suppliers Customers Peers

How your chosen interviewers handle the logistics is another consideration. Perhaps you've already decided that a multi-interviewer approach is beneficial, and you've determined your interviewers. But will each interviewer question each candidate separately, or will two or more interviewers sit down together with each candidate to question him?

Take a look at the different methods of interviewing within the multi-interviewer approach, and the pros and cons of each. You may wind up using a combination to get your best results.

Interview Method: Individual

Description: One-on-one

Pros: Focuses data

Cons: Takes time

Interview Method: Pair

Description: Two-on-one

Pros: Saves time, makes data consistent

Cons: May make candidate uncomfortable, the two may not complement each other well

---

Interview Method: Group

Description: Three-to-eight-on-one

Pros: Saves time, adds to reliability of data, response to one question may stimulate others

Cons: May intimidate, candidate may not act *"normally,"* *(candidate may be good at responding to panel, but not good at position)*

If you are unsure as to which method to select, use the following guidelines:

♦ Individual interviews are best for situations where the interviewer will be the supervisor of the candidate.

♦ The pair method works well when a candidate is being interviewed by future peers.

♦ The group method is appropriate when you are seeking customer/supplier input.

Regardless of the method you choose, you will need to coordinate the questions that will be asked by each interviewer. Divide your list of performance-based questions that you created on the Performance-Based Interview Questions Worksheet among the interviewers.

If you choose to have interviewers question each candidate separately, you may want to have different interviewers ask a core question, and then compare results. This may be useful in assessing the consistency of a candidate's response. Try not to overuse this technique, however (*no candidate wants to answer the same question over and over again, and it limits what you learn about him*).

Provide each of the interviewers with a numbered list of the performance-based questions. In addition, each interviewer will get an Interview Notes sheet for recording responses and rating them. On the Interview Notes, you must list the numbers of the performance-based questions each interviewer will be asking, and room is provided for a response and a rating for each question. In addition, you and the other interviewers will provide a recommendation of whether you should hire the candidate, and you'll write a rationale for that recommendation.

If you are using two or more interviewers at a time, be sure to go over basic turn-taking rules, so you don't step on each other's toes.

Bear in mind that interviewing can be stressful for both the candidate and the interviewer. Having well-coordinated logistics helps to reduce tension. Decide which of your multiple interviewers will be the best person to ask each of your performance-based questions. Choose where the interviews will be conducted. If it is a shared space, such as a conference room, be sure and book it for that day.

These things may seem like trivial details, but, when overlooked, can significantly disrupt the interview. Once again, it all boils down to preparation and planning. Good preparation and communication, performed *in advance*, will help to ensure a good interview and a great new employee.

At Mother Earth, Inc.,...

Anika isolated herself in the small conference room with her large stack of resumes, a pen, a pad of sticky notes, and a jumbo coffee, and settled down to work.

She emerged much later, with the results of her efforts: three stacks, labeled A *(seventeen resumes)*, B *(twenty-two resumes)*, and C *(eighty-three resumes)*. Then she approached Greg Chandler, the Marketing Department manager who had previously assisted her in designing the functions and responsibilities for the position, and who had come up with some terrific performance-based questions.

"Greg, I know you're always busy, but would you mind setting aside a little time to check over my first pass at screening these resumes?" Anika asked.

"Sure, Anika, I'll look at them tomorrow. I've got a meeting in the afternoon, but my morning's free," Greg replied.

Anika quickly explained the A-B-C system. The next morning, she and Greg whittled down the stacks to eight resumes in pile A, sixteen in pile B, and ninety-eight in pile C. Anika thanked Greg for his valuable input in screening the resumes.

Since Anika had already contacted Mother Earth's benefits coordinator, Pat Bennington, and an innovative copywriter in the Marketing Department, Martin Grant, about doing the phone screening, she needed to prep the resumes and route them to these two.

Using the Phone Screen Organizer, she jotted down questions regarding technical skills and other requirements that were not listed on the resume. One applicant had listed secondary education at both the University of Washington and Gonzaga University, but had not made mention of a bachelor's degree. Another listed proficiency in software that was a less sophisticated version of the one used by Mother Earth, so Anika was unsure if the applicant would be comfortable using their current software.

She attached a list of questions to each resume, and split up the piles evenly, retaining one pile for herself. Both Pat and Martin committed to finishing the screens within two days, so Anika decided not to worry about them and get her own task done.

She found out that two applicants had already been hired elsewhere. Three others did not meet her requirements. She would have to contact one applicant after-hours and another was out of town until the weekend. One candidate, Lizbeth, seemed promising. She had been an intern in the Marketing Department of a soft-drink manufacturer for a couple of semesters during her college studies and had been working in her present position as an administrative assistant for five years.

SCREENING YOUR APPLICANTS

Anika found through the phone screen that the organization, a healthcare provider, used not only the same software as Mother Earth, but the same phone system. She also gleaned the *"bonus information"* that the organization was downsizing on all levels, so Lizbeth would be available for training soon.

Anika wondered how Pat and Martin were doing.

Finally, you are a little closer to those all-important interviews. Use the following tip sheet to help you prepare for the face-to-face interviewing that should lead to selecting a successful candidate.

Key Tips

1. Make sure each interviewer knows what questions to ask.

2. Check that all interview room(s) are reserved.

3. Give each candidate directions to the interview location.

4. Double-check flight information and accommodations, if applicable.

5. Put everything in writing (*minds have been known to slip on occasion; besides, if, for any reason, an interviewer can't make it, you'll have all the necessary information*).

6. Include a copy of each candidate's resume with each set of questions (*DO NOT write on the resume itself*).

With the phone screens completed, and your interviews set up, you're practically halfway through the Performance-Based Selection Process. Interviewing is next on your agenda. Just think: soon, you'll be meeting your chosen candidates face-to-face.

44   INTERVIEWING AND SELECTING HIGH PERFORMERS

CHAPTER FOUR WORKSHEET: IMPROVING YOUR PHONE-SCREENING TECHNIQUES

1. List some questions you plan to ask when conducting your phone screen.

_____

_____

_____

_____

_____

_____

_____

_____

_____

_____

_____

_____

_____

_____

2. Describe the methods of interviewing you have used in the past. Which method do you believe would be most helpful for any of your upcoming interviews? Why?

_____

_____

_____

_____

_____

_____

_____

_____

_____

_____

_____

_____

_____

_____

_____

3. Before you begin your interviews, ensure that you have prepared adequately by checking the following tips:

Key Tips

☐ 1. Make sure each interviewer knows what questions to ask.

☐ 2. Check that all interview room(s) are reserved.

☐ 3. Give each candidate directions to the interview location.

☐ 4. Double-check flight information and accommodations, if applicable.

☐ 5. Put everything in writing (*minds have been known to default on occasion; besides, if, for any reason, an interviewer can't make it, you'll have all the necessary information*).

☐ 6. Include a copy of each candidate's resume with each set of questions (*DO NOT write on the resume itself*).

INTERVIEWING YOUR CANDIDATES

 At last. You have reached the heart of the selection process and the interviews are at hand. Luckily, you have been following the systematic process in this guidebook, and are already prepared for this important step.

In the preparation step, you came up with numerous performance-based questions to ask during interviewing. And, in the screening step, you've been able to narrow the field down to about five or six viable candidates whom you will interview.

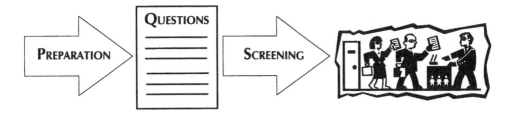

In this interviewing step, you'll be:

 ☑ Gathering job-related data from your candidates,

 ☑ Providing each candidate with information, and

 ☑ Wrapping up the interview by discussing the next steps.

This interviewing step will be easier, because you have done your homework. However, here are some *"interview do's"* to keep in mind. Take a moment to reflect on these underlying guidelines before you begin your interviews.

Interviewing Do's:

♦ **Show respect at all times.**
Candidates are not only fellow human beings, but potential customers. Treat them accordingly.

♦ **Listen a great deal, responding when necessary.**
Candidates should do most of the talking (about 75-80 percent).

♦ **Probe for validation.**
Use follow-up questions to ask for specific experiences that link to the behavior or trait you are searching for.

♦ **Maintain control of the interview.**
Carefully guide the interview so that it stays on track and within appropriate time limits.

You may be tired of hearing this, but it pays to mention it again—prepare! Don't make yourself appear disorganized by shuffling through papers or awkwardly reading the resume while the candidate sits in embarrassed silence. Be at ease and familiar with what should happen during an interview before you begin.

Gather Job-Related Data From Your Candidates

Your initial aim during the interview is to get answers to those all-important performance-based questions. This isn't an interrogation, however. Launch into the interview gracefully by establishing rapport with the candidate.

Greet the candidate positively, and use her name. At this point, you are the lone representative of your organization. Exhibit common courtesy: provide the candidate with a comfortable place to sit and a place for her belongings. If appropriate, ask the candidate about her trip, the suitability of her accommodations, or another topic of mutual interest.

Let the small talk continue on this basis for a short time, to let the candidate settle in and relax. As you transition into the interview itself, build on the rapport you have established by sending positive signals: smile, lean forward, be open, and use direct eye contact whenever possible.

Begin by explaining how the interview will be conducted. This will make the candidate feel more comfortable, and she will know what to expect. For example, if your candidate's name is Susan, you might say:

"We're going to be together for about an hour today, Susan. You're going to do most of the talking, and I'll do most of the listening. I'll also be taking some notes. We'll be spending about forty-five minutes on your background, and then we'll switch, and I'll tell you a little bit about our company. Then I'll answer any of your questions."

This is also the time to discuss the multiple-interviewer approach you'll be using. Tell your candidates whom they will be meeting. Keep everything in the open.

Letting the candidate know that you will be taking notes throughout the interview helps to reduce anxiety. You have provided yourself and your selected interviewers with a list of questions and an Interview Notes sheet. On the Interview Notes sheet are the numbers of the questions each interviewer is to ask. You might choose to highlight your interviewers' particular questions on their list of performance-based questions. Doing so will make the interview run smoother.

Run down your list of selected nontechnical performance-based questions, clarifying and probing for further information when necessary. Use active listening techniques, such as checking for understanding and paraphrasing the content of the candidate's response to ensure accuracy.

Don't let your list of performance-based questions limit the scope of your interview. It's a good jumping-off point, and may open up avenues of additional interest that can help you through the selection process. You can gain this additional information through the use of "*probes*"—phrases that encourage a candidate to reveal more information on a particular topic.

Some sample probes are listed below:

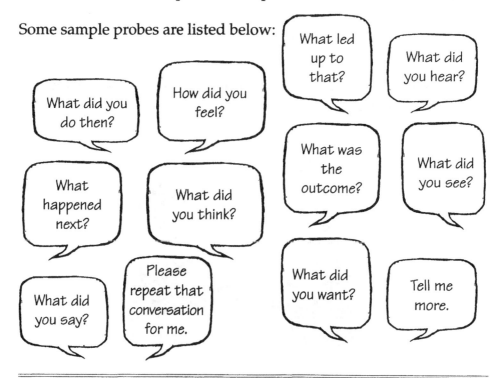

Don't probe for further answers until a candidate is through with his initial answer. Unless, that is, the candidate is going off on a tangent. Then use a nonverbal signal *(nod, raised hand, change of facial expression)*, to encourage the candidate to pause, so you can use a probe to keep the interview on track.

As you gather information from the candidate, don't neglect to observe the candidate's nonverbal communication, as well. Is the candidate at ease, self-assured? If one of the demonstrated behaviors or traits you are seeking is decisiveness, are you getting an overall impression of decisiveness from the candidate's demeanor?

Lastly, do your candidates' *"words"* mesh with their *"music"*? In other words, do the claims of the candidates appear to be in line with the behavior that they exhibit? How believable is a candidate who claims to have extensive experience in public speaking, yet speaks poorly and uses bad grammar? List all responses on your Interview Notes sheet, whether positive or negative. Then you can make a recommendation and can compare notes with your fellow interviewers later.

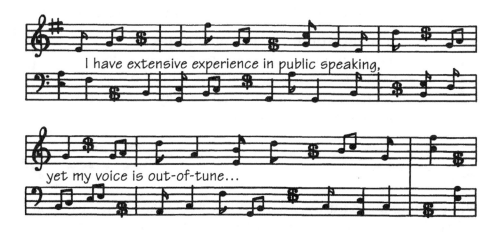

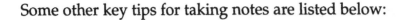

Some other key tips for taking notes are listed below:

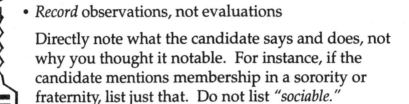

- *Record* observations, not evaluations

  Directly note what the candidate says and does, not why you thought it notable. For instance, if the candidate mentions membership in a sorority or fraternity, list just that. Do not list *"sociable."*

- *Record* behavior each time it is observed

  If a candidate references a particular behavior repeatedly, keep track of it. This will come in handy when you evaluate and make a recommendation on the candidate. One easy method is to place a check mark next to your initial notation each time it is repeated.

- *Record* notes so they will not be readable by your candidate

  Your candidate may be distracted if your notes are easily readable. Minimize the time you spend looking at the page, and keep your note pad from being seen.

- *Pause* a moment before recording your observations

  If you begin writing directly after a specific comment, your candidate will be clued in as to what you are recording. Maintain a brief pause before recording your notes, and always look at the candidate when asking a direct question.

While taking notes during an interview may seem awkward, it is definitely preferable to trusting your memory. You probably have had some experience taking notes *(e.g., during classes, meetings, or presentations)*. In time, taking reliable notes during interviews will become second nature.

Your completed Interview Notes sheet should look something like this:

INTERVIEW NOTES		
Name of Interviewer: Mary Pinoza		Date: February 9, XXXX
Name of Candidate: Thomas Jones		Position: Graphic Designer
QUESTION #:	RESPONSE TO QUESTIONS	RATING (1-5) 1 = Not a fit 5 = Excellent fit
# 2 (What have you done when you've found yourself swamped?)	Asked for extension	1
# 5 (What are you looking for in this job that you didn't find in your last job?)	Challenges	5
# 6 (How do you react to rumors on the job?)	Share with other to verify	2

ADDITIONAL COMMENTS:

Prefers flex hours, enjoys organizing company functions, willing to work weekends/long hours

Final recommendation: ☐ **Hire** ☒ **Don't Hire**

RATIONALE:

Enthusiasm and willingness are there, but candidate needs to learn delegating skills to fit in with our organization.

In addition to gathering information regarding your needs for the position, you need to get a clear idea of what your candidates want from the organization. Focus in on their interests, needs, and concerns. This information will help you to determine if the position will ultimately satisfy your candidates.

Provide Each Candidate With Information

Even though one of your aims is to let your candidates do most of the talking, at some point you will have to describe the position and your organization, as well as answer your candidates' questions.

Again, remember that you are representing your organization. Be accessible and create a positive impression of the position and the overall working atmosphere. Take this chance to show your enthusiasm about the environment you work in. Describe the organizational values, culture, and expectations.

You may need to explain exactly what your organization or division does. Create an accurate picture of the position within the organization, and the way in which the position relates to other departments. Be especially clear when covering the prospects for advancements and the level of authority the position will involve.

Also, describe any positions reporting to the open job, as well as detailing who the candidate would be expected to interact with on a regular basis.

You may also inform the candidate about the *"perks"* that would apply to the position *(highlight the benefit packages, discount on company products, etc.)*. In addition, you may give a quick tour of the office or department the candidate would occupy, if you have enough time to do so.

Encourage the candidate to ask questions, and provide thoughtful responses. Despite all the information you have already provided, your candidate most likely will still have concerns or need to clarify certain issues. Interviewing is a two-way street. Not only do you need to approve of the candidate, the candidate needs to obtain information in order to decide if this is the right position for him or her.

Again, you must control the flow of the interview by not allowing this part of the interview to take too much time. This is especially important, since your use of the multi-interviewer approach may call for you to pass the candidate on to the next interviewer at a specific time. Keep a discreet eye on the clock, gently nudging the candidate into the next step if you are beginning to run behind schedule.

 Hot Tip: *Mount a clock on the wall just behind where your candidate will be seated; this way you won't be caught glancing at your wristwatch.*

Wrap Up The Interview By Discussing The Next Steps

You've questioned your candidate, and given information about the position and your organization. You've also answered any questions your candidate has had. Now you must wrap up the interview.

Begin by briefly summarizing the key issues you discussed during the interview. Not only does this provide a sense of closure, it also allows you and the candidate to review any remaining action items required.

Some action items on your list might be:

☑ Providing a list of references

☑ Testing for technical skills

☑ Providing a copy of a license or documents

☑ Setting up another interview

Once you feel the candidate has a clear picture of the organization, the position, and what action items you require, let him in on what will happen next.

Since you are using the Performance-Based Selection Process, it is certainly appropriate for you to tell your candidates that you will be selecting a final candidate soon. Let your candidates know, within a specified time range, when they will be hearing from you.

However, don't discuss your *"evaluation"* of the candidate at the end of the interview. You don't know how the other interviewers will evaluate each candidate.

You can provide a way for the candidate to contact you or the organization. Again, this choice is a personal one. Some interviewers feel comfortable handing over their business card with their direct line noted, while others prefer any calls to be handled by an assistant or at the front desk. Keep in mind that certain desirable behaviors or traits you are seeking *(e.g., persistence in a salesperson)*, can surface in the form of repeated phone calls asking *"Did I get the job?"*

"Did I get the job?"

Since you are using the multi-interviewer approach, you may designate one of the other interviewers as a contact for any follow-up questions.

Before you escort the candidate to the door, or the next interviewer, be sure to thank him or her. And, if you have promised to do so, give the candidate a brief tour of the office or department.

At Mother Earth, Inc.,...

Anika, Pat, and Martin met after two days to discuss the results of their phone screening. Anika had found one other promising applicant besides Lizbeth, but she still had not made contact with the out-of-town candidate. Pat found three applicants who were qualified; Martin found two.

Anika wasted no time in contacting the colleagues she had chosen to assist her in conducting the interviews: Thalia Harcourt, Greg Chandler's executive secretary, and Dan Morrissey, who held the receptionist position before Anika, and was now working in Distribution. After coordinating the days they had available for interviewing, she passed the candidate list off to Pat, who had volunteered to set up the interviews. In the meantime, Anika continued to try contacting the one remaining applicant.

"Okay, everything's set," Pat said, dropping the interview schedule on Anika's desk. *"Remember, Anika, you owe me one."*

"No problem, Pat," Anika responded. *"I really appreciate your help. You truly go above and beyond..."*

The next day, Anika reviewed her list of questions and her Interview Notes sheet while she waited for Eric, a candidate whom Martin had contacted by phone, to arrive. Finally, she looked up to see an anxious young man, who appeared somewhat lost. She noted that it was almost ten minutes past their appointed nine o'clock meeting time.

She stood to greet Eric, and shook hands warmly. He immediately began apologizing. *"I am usually never late,"* Eric said, *"but the parking structure you specified for me to park in was full, and I had to hunt around for an alternate. I ended up about three blocks away,"* he gasped.

Anika mentally slapped her forehead. *"Shoot, I always get here so early, I never have a problem finding a spot. I forgot how a lot of the late-comers and merchants have been complaining lately,"* she thought. Aloud, she said, *"Eric, I do apologize for the oversight. Would you care for a glass of water or some coffee?"*

He declined both offers politely, so Anika guided him to a chair, indicating the coat rack for his overcoat and umbrella. *"Seems like 'wet' is the only kind of weather we're ever going to have,"* she commented. *"What's new?"* Eric responded. *"I've lived in Seattle for five years and have gone through at least five umbrellas."* The two of them laughed.

After they'd broken the ice, Anika explained that she would be taking notes throughout the interview. She said that they would spend about forty-five minutes to an hour together, before Eric would meet with two other interviewers. Eric settled in and looked serious.

As she launched into her performance-based questions, Anika maintained eye contact and took discreet notes. She clarified and probed as she went along, finding out that Eric had actually had a small part in setting up trade shows at his last position.

She also found out that he was just a few credits short of getting his master's degree, and made a note to be sure and tell Eric about the organization's fund-matching program for continuing education. He seemed genuinely enthusiastic about Mother Earth, Inc., and grew even more so as Anika described the position and the policies of the organization. By the time she ushered him out the door, she had to restrain herself from offering him the job on the spot.

She immediately went to Pat's office, and asked her to phone the other candidates to inform them of alternate parking arrangements. *"I'd do it myself, only I've got another candidate waiting for me,"* she explained.

"Yeah, yeah...don't forget I'm keeping track of all this stuff," Pat muttered.

At the end of the day, Anika had completed four of the seven interviews that had been set up. She uttered silent thanks for her Interview Notes. Without them, the day would have been a total scramble. In a couple of days, she'd have to compare her notes with those of her colleagues.

CHAPTER FIVE WORKSHEET:
CONDUCTING THE INTERVIEW

1. Using the sample Interview Notes sheet below, assign a rating next to each response. If the candidate's overall rating is above 3, make the recommendation to hire and state your rationale. If 3 or below, make the recommendation to not hire, again stating your rationale for doing so.

INTERVIEW NOTES		
QUESTION #:	**RESPONSE TO QUESTIONS**	**RATING (1-5)** 1 = Not a fit 5 = Excellent fit
1. How do you start a typical work day?	Go through appointments and TO DO list.	
2. If we were to call your last employer, what would she/he say about how you worked with others?	Had problem supervisor and members of support staff.	
3. What do you normally do when your schedule is disrupted?	React to situation, then try to make up time after hours.	
4. How do you decide on whom to ask for advice?	Usually select from peers before approaching supervisor.	
5. What are some of the things that motivated you in your last job?	Positive feedback of boss, advancement, promotion.	

ADDITIONAL COMMENTS:

Final recommendation: ☐ Hire ☐ Don't Hire

RATIONALE:

2. What do you like best about your organization? List these things below:

_____

_____

_____

_____

_____

_____

_____

_____

_____

_____

_____

_____

_____

_____

_____

_____

3. How will you address *"difficult"* questions from candidates concerning organization-specific issues (*e.g., a tradition of a 50-60 hour work week, a very authorcratic CEO, not-so-family-friendly policies, etc.*).

QUESTION	WAYS TO ADDRESS

SELECTING YOUR FINAL CANDIDATE

 Well, you're getting closer. But getting closer to the end of the Performance-Based Selection Process doesn't mean you can coast. Selecting your final candidate, while an exciting prospect, also demands careful attention.

In this selecting step, you'll be:

☑ Conducting the assessment of technical skills,

☑ Completing a Candidate Comparison Sheet, and

☑ Conducting reference checks on the final top candidates.

These tasks are essential to selecting a high performer. You may want to ask your fellow interviewers for their help with the tasks in this step.

Conduct The Assessment Of Technical Skills

During phone screening and interviewing, you asked about the technical skills required to fulfill the position. Now it's time to see if your top candidates can *"walk the walk"* as well as *"talk the talk."*

Part of your preparation work called for you to determine the method of testing the technical skills for the position you have available. To review, your basic options are:

1. Interview by expert
2. Testing
3. In-basket assessment

Your organization may require additional types of evaluation *(such as physical lifting requirements or drug screening)*, but at this point you need only be concerned about the testing that applies to technical skills. *(The additional tests are usually handled by Human Resources staff or others.)*

In the interest of conserving time, you may wish to have your candidates tested on the same day they are interviewed, or you may wish to only schedule tests for the final candidates who still rate as possible hires after the interviews.

Some organizations routinely test each group of applicants prior to the interviews, as part of the screening process. While this may seem logical at first glance, it really isn't time- or cost-effective. Your primary goal is to choose candidates whose past behavior predicts a good fit within your organization. Then, and only then, should you test their technical skills. A poor fit *(regardless of technical skills)* will still prove to be a poor fit.

Back at Mother Earth, Inc.,...

The interviews were finally over. Even though it was only three days, it felt like two weeks to Anika. In addition to the parking mishap, one candidate decided to show up for the interview despite a hacking cough, and another had managed to spill a cup of coffee on her desk. Was it always like this?

Anika collected the Interview Notes sheets from her fellow interviewers, Thalia Harcourt and Dan Morrissey. Anika was especially anxious to receive Dan's comments, since he had also held the receptionist position, and, next to Anika, was most aware of what the position demanded.

Due to the number of interviews, and the fact that Anika had decided to conduct part of the testing herself, she set up testing for a later date with the candidates who had successfully passed the interviews. She collected everyone's interview materials immediately in order to determine who should go on to be tested.

As she scanned the completed Interview Notes, she was relieved to discover that both Thalia and Dan shared her opinion to definitely not hire one candidate. On another, they were divided 2-1 against one candidate, with Anika giving her recommendation to hire. Upon review of her Interview Notes, Anika decided to cast her vote along with the others, realizing that she had felt sorry for the candidate at the time of the interview *(due to the spilt coffee)* and rated her a bit high. She reviewed her recommendations with Thalia and Dan in a short meeting.

Now the field was down to five. Of these, they jointly decided on the three candidates whom they would schedule for testing. They based their decision on each candidate's initial overall rating and any other supporting data that had been brought out in the interview.

"Okay, so I'll be calling in Lizbeth, Eric, and Cheryl for testing. Are we all agreed?" Anika asked, getting up from the table.

"That's right, but do you know what kinds of tests you'll be running?" Dan asked.

"It's in the bag," Anika replied. *"I've got a couple of innovative tests worked out that should give us the information we need."*

"What if nobody passes the tests?" Thalia asked.

"Then we test our two back-up candidates, right, Anika?" Dan asked.

"You bet. I feel pretty confident, though, that I'm holding the winning candidate's form in my hand." Anika walked out the door....

The results of your technical skills evaluations should be fairly simple to interpret. Sometimes, such as with an English or grammar test, it is best to test on a pass/fail basis. For highly technical skills, a percentage or numerical test result can better pinpoint the level of skill.

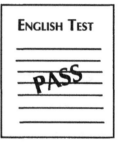

Once your successful candidates have been tested, you will plug their scores into a Candidate Comparison Sheet, along with the overall ratings from their interviews. The results will bring you closer to selecting your final candidate.

Complete The Candidate Comparison Sheet

You've gathered data from a wide variety of sources; now you're just about ready to analyze it, using your comparison tool. It's not quite as sophisticated as it sounds. Basically, you will be transferring each candidate's data onto a Candidate Comparison Sheet. Unlike your Interview Notes, on which you evaluated each candidate individually, the Candidate Comparison Sheet is a tool designed to highlight the strengths and weaknesses of each candidate in relation to each other.

CANDIDATE COMPARISON SHEET

N: Name C: Last Company/Position S: Last Annual Salary O: Other Compensation Y: Years Of Direct Experience	Candidate #1 N: C: S: O: Y:	Candidate #2 N: C: S: O: Y:	Candidate #3 N: C: S: O: Y:
Test Score			
Test Score			
Overall Rating—Question # 1			
Overall Rating—Question # 2			
Overall Rating—Question # 3			
Overall Rating—Question # 4			
Overall Rating—Question # 5			
Overall Rating—Question # 6			
(Other:)			
Overall Interview Rating			
Rank Order			

Don't be intimidated by all these references to tools, however. The real "*tool*" in evaluation and comparison is your keen mind and your sharp observation skills.

The task before you is to review each interviewer's Interview Notes and come up with an overall evaluation for each candidate. Your overall evaluation is important, as it will form the basis of comparison of the final candidates. Before you begin, get into the correct mindset by recognizing the following underlying principles:

General Principles Of Evaluation

1. **Evaluation is an inherently subjective process**

   While you may strive for complete objectivity, it can still be overshadowed by bias. This is why the multiple-interviewer approach is so important—others can recognize and point out a bias you didn't even know you had.

2. **The apparent qualities of your candidates may not coincide with their true qualities**

   As good as the performance-based questions you designed are, the candidate still controls what information you receive during the interview. Take that information with "*a grain of salt*," recognizing that your candidates probably appear to be just a little better than they really are.

3. **Established patterns of behavior are the best predictors of future behavior**

   Behavior observed only once, by one person, cannot accurately predict future behavior. Behavioral evidence must be gathered about candidates from a variety of situations. This is why the multi-interviewer approach is a must.

4. Consider the *"whole person"*

Each candidate will have strengths and weaknesses that vary amongst the behaviors and traits, technical skills, and other requirements that you have specified. You may find yourself wishing to create that perfect candidate using the best aspects of each! In reality, you'll end up accepting the best mix of these elements, even though some areas will need improvement.

Keep in mind that evaluation and comparison are two completely different things. Initially, during and after the interview, you evaluated each candidate using your Interview Notes. You rated each according to the same absolute standard (*i.e., the technical skills and other requirements you listed on your Performance Requirements Worksheet, and the behaviors or traits you identified when you designed your performance-based questions*).

Candidate # 1	Candidate # 2	Candidate # 3
Judgment ✩✩	Judgment ✩	Judgment ✩✩✩✩
Organization ✩	Organization ✩✩✩	Organization ✩✩
Leadership ✩✩✩	Leadership ✩	Leadership ✩✩✩✩
Flexibility ✩✩	Flexibility ✩✩✩✩	Flexibility ✩

Now, you will rate each candidate based on a *"relative"* standard by using the Candidate Comparison Sheet. Keep the completed sheet in a safe place, since you'll need it when you begin to rank your final candidates.

However, before you actually begin to rank the candidates, you should determine the decision-making option you will be using. Make your choice from the following three most commonly used decision-making options.

Unanimous Decision

Best used for a *"critical"* or *"high-profile"* position. If many people will have to work with the new hire, you should try for a unanimous decision.

Pros:
Increases likelihood of good fit. Increases team commitment to the candidate.

Cons:
Difficult to get everyone to agree on one person. May have to reject a good candidate.

Majority Decision
Best used for most jobs.

Pros:
Generally allows for a good decision. Gives interviewers a feeling of participation.

Cons:
May accept a candidate not agreeable to all. Interviewers may not work well with chosen candidate (*if they did not favor him/her*).

Input-Only Decision
Best used if manager or main interviewer understands the position well, or if position involves limited contact with others.

Pros:
Quickest decision-making method. Interviewers can speak freely.

Cons:
Interviewers may resent lack of a *"vote."* Again, interviewers may not work well with chosen candidate (*if they did not favor him/her*).

If you choose to use the *"Unanimous"* or *"Majority"* decision-making option, you should schedule a meeting to rank the candidates. This meeting may include your fellow interviewers, testers, and screeners. If possible, use an overhead projector to graphically exhibit the Candidate Comparison Sheet to all, or prepare handouts so each person has a copy to work from.

Use the Candidate Comparison Sheet to establish a rank order for your top three candidates. This will determine not only your top-rated candidate, but whom you will contact next, should your offer be rejected or break down for some other reason.

As you and the group look at the sheet, allow plenty of time for discussion and voting. If you are using the *"Unanimous"* option, you may need to poll the group many times. If an agreement cannot be reached, you will need to interview more candidates.

If you use the *"Majority"* option, only one voting session should be necessary.

If you have decided to use the *"Input-Only"* option, you may opt to schedule a brief meeting to discuss and validate your ranking decision or talk to the interviewers individually. In either case, you need to inform the colleagues that assisted you of your decision, thanking them for their input and effort.

Mother Earth, Inc.,...

Anika studied the results of the completed word-processing tests for Lizbeth, Eric, and Cheryl. To her surprise, Lizbeth did not do as well as either Cheryl or Eric. Cheryl was definitely a whiz, with a 100 percent accuracy rate on the spreadsheet. Her sample memo was perfect as well. Eric was competitive, with just one minor flaw in the memo. Both Eric and Cheryl had passed the phone test, but again, Lizbeth had lagged behind. Alongside his *"fail"* comment, Carl had noted *"Lizbeth failed to connect 4 out of 12 calls!"*

Even with the superior results of her interviews, it was clear that Lizbeth would be ranked in last position. The results seemed less obvious when it came to ranking Cheryl and Eric. Anika had plugged their test results into the Candidate Comparison Sheet, along with Lizbeth's. Then she made an overhead transparency of the sheet and rounded up her colleagues for one final meeting.

Since this was her first effort at hiring, Anika had decided to go with the *"Majority"* option to make the final ranking decision. She also decided to call on all the people who had helped her in the process thus far and get their input.

Pat, Martin, Dan, Thalia, and Carl gathered at the conference table. Unfortunately, Greg was out of town, but said his vote would be available in case of a tie. They scanned the Candidate Comparison Sheet that was projected on the screen. All agreed that Lizbeth would be their third choice.

"Even though Cheryl scored higher on the technical stuff, I think Eric is a better match with our organization," Pat stated.

"I disagree. I want a person in the receptionist position who can turn in a perfect memo the first time and doesn't make mistakes on spreadsheets. I strongly favor Cheryl," Martin stated.

"But Eric clearly has what it takes to refine his job skills. The way he would add value to our organization lies in his strong customer service skills," Dan remarked.

After the debate had continued for a while, Anika polled the group. Eric barely passed Cheryl in holding the first-rated position. Cheryl would be the back-up, and Lizbeth would be next in line.

"Okay, can everybody live with this?" Anika asked. The group gave a positive response, even Martin.

"Then I'll get busy checking references, and it will be a done deal," Anika said.

The group heaved a collective sigh of relief....

Once rank order is established, you'll have a clear picture of your top three candidates. Obviously, the candidate at the top of your list will get your offer first. However, before you start putting that offer together, there is one final task for you to complete.

Conduct Reference Checks On Your Top Candidates

Reference checking is your final opportunity to ensure that you extend your job offer to the right candidate. In most cases, the information you get by checking references really doesn't tell you a lot of new information about your candidates' past performance. However, it does serve to confirm or deny what you have learned so far, and can, in the worst-case scenario, reveal any number of *"red flags"* that might affect your hiring decision.

The amount and content of information a former employer can provide about a past employee can be constrained by law. And who actually conducts the reference check is oftentimes strictly controlled by organizational policy. Some high-security positions require a background check. This involves getting *"character information"* from friends or family members and running a check for past criminal activity. If this is required, your organization should have a qualified person to do this.

If your organization mandates that reference checks must be conducted by the Human Resources or legal staff, you should only hand off candidate information and await the results. If you have the freedom to conduct reference checks yourself, be careful to observe some commonsense boundaries.

Your candidates may have included a list of references on their resumes, or your organization may have a space on the job application for this information. If reference information is not already in your hands, contact your top candidates by phone to ask for this information.

The best person for you to contact would be the candidate's last or current immediate supervisor. If you are able to speak with this person, you should be able to get the most informative feedback regarding the candidate. Again, policies vary from organization to organization; you may be referred to someone in the Human Resources Department. Try for the immediate supervisor first, since Human Resources will not be able to give you as much firsthand information.

You may also wish to verify information regarding education, licensing, and bonding prior to extending an offer. Again, look for the person who would have had the most contact with your candidate.

No matter who the contact person is, keep your questions brief and bias-free. Be careful to avoid questions that are not job-related. If the person you are speaking with begins providing any information that is not job-related, it is up to you to tactfully move on to other subjects. Keep the conversation focused at all times.

Your basic reference check should go somewhat along these lines:

1. Obtain reference information from candidate. Double-check to ensure you have your candidate's permission to conduct reference checks.

2. Attempt to contact a previous supervisor, rather than the Human Resources Department.

3. Introduce yourself and your organization. Explain that the candidate is applying for a position within your organization and that you would like to conduct a reference check. Ask if it is a convenient time to do so.

4. Be sure to mention that the call will be kept in strictest confidence, and point out that any information given will benefit not only the candidate, but your organization.

5. If their organizational policy does not allow for reference checking, ask if they will simply verify employment. *(You may be able to push for additional information, such as job title, last salary, and name of supervisor.)*

6. Once you have consent, give your contact person an opportunity to gather files or other information.

7. Briefly describe the position and what performance-based behaviors you're looking for.

8. Ask your questions in a non-biased way *(e.g., "How did the candidate handle meeting deadlines?" instead of "Did he/she have a problem meeting deadlines?").*

9. Thank the individual and organization for any assistance received.

Reference checking is oftentimes useful if you are having trouble ranking your candidates. You may also uncover some information that could lead you to question your candidates' statements. If this should occur, be sure and give your candidates the opportunity to clarify any questionable issues.

Testing and assessment of technical skills has helped to fill out your candidates' profiles. The Candidate Comparison Sheet has helped you to create a rank order of your top three candidates. Reference checking has helped to fill in the blanks and verify information. Now it is time to make an offer.

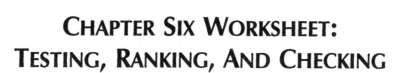

CHAPTER SIX WORKSHEET:
TESTING, RANKING, AND CHECKING

1. Study the list of positions below. What type of testing for technical skills would be the best choice for each position? List your choice below and state why you feel that way.

Position: Assistant Controller

Test:_____

Why?_____

Position: Customer Service Representative

Test:_____

Why?_____

Position: Word Processing Supervisor

Test:_____

Why?_____

Position: Corporate Trust Administrator

Test:_____

Why?_____

Position: Avionics Engineer

Test:_____

Why?_____

2. Think about two different positions within your organization. Would you be willing to hire candidates who had all the behaviors and traits needed to fulfill the positions, but weaker technical skills? Why or why not?

Position # 1:_____

Hire/Don't Hire:_____

Why/Why Not: _____

_____

_____

_____

_____

_____

Position # 2:_____

Hire/Don't Hire:_____

Why/Why Not: _____

_____

_____

_____

_____

_____

3. What would be your next step if you received one strong
negative response and two positive responses when conducting
a reference check on a candidate? Why?

_____

_____

_____

_____

_____

_____

_____

_____

_____

_____

_____

_____

_____

_____

_____

_____

_____

OFFERING YOUR FINAL CANDIDATE THE POSITION

You have reached the final step of the Performance-Based Selection Process. So far, you have pretty much had control of the process—preparing, screening, interviewing, and testing have all been in your hands. Now it's time to hand over some of the control to your first-choice candidate. Although you play a major role in this step, your final candidate gets to make the choice of whether or not to join your organization.

This doesn't mean your job is over. You still have several important decisions to make. In addition, you need to tie up loose ends with all who applied for the position. In this offering step, you'll be:

☑ Determining offer components,

☑ Making a verbal and a written offer, and

☑ Informing non-selected candidates of your decision.

Don't ease up now. How you behave in carrying out this last step will reflect not only upon you, but upon your entire organization.

Determine Offer Components

You've got a complex and delicate decision to make. You must put together an offer that is attractive enough to get your first-choice candidate on board, but you must not violate internal equity. Your offer must be competitive with the external market, but also consistent with your organization's Human Resources practices. In short, you need help!

Luckily, Human Resources should be able to help you out. Seek input from the internal experts in your organization. They can provide insight as to what level of compensation employees in similar positions with similar experience get. The last thing you want to do is alienate other workers by offering a salary that is too high. In addition, the benefits package you offer should be consistent with your organization's current policy and appropriate for the level of the open position.

Your offer needn't necessarily be *"equal"* to that of current employees, but it should be *"equitable."* It should also be in line with the current market. Review any external information you can get your hands on, whether it's information gleaned from business journals or from personal contacts in other organizations. Once again, Human Resources may be able to provide you with a survey of salaries paid in the market.

If you don't have access to an internal Human Resources professional, consider the following to develop a competitive, yet equitable offer.

1. Hire an external Human Resources consultant.

   The consultant can survey the market or gather data concerning current compensation rates. In either case, you will make a better decision with accurate information.

2. Call a trade or professional association related to the open position.

   These organizations may sponsor or conduct salary and benefit surveys, and usually the results are available to their members.

3. Research information collected by the government.

   The Bureau of Labor Statistics collects a great deal of compensation information. Draw upon this rich source of data when developing your job offer.

Make A Verbal And A Written Offer

Once you've gathered all the information you need, put together the offer. For legal reasons, it is best to put your offer in writing *(in an offer letter)*; then verbally extend the offer by reading the contents of your offer letter to the candidate. This will help ensure no misunderstandings between yourself and the candidate. The verbal offer also is used to *"sell"* the candidate on taking the position.

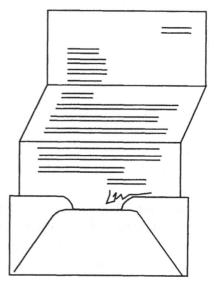

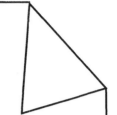

A comprehensive offer letter should include:

1. Position title and reporting relationships

2. Base salary

3. Start date and location

4. Overview of "perks," such as benefits, retirement plan (e.g., 401K plan, etc.), profit sharing, childcare compensation or on-site care, etc. (don't go into detail, however—all these items will be explained thoroughly when the new employee receives his or her benefits package at the time of hire)

5. Sign-on bonus, if applicable

6. Vacation time/"personal days" policy

7. Relocation reimbursement, if applicable

8. Statement of contingencies (e.g., hiring is contingent upon passing a drug screen, etc.)

9. Space for candidate's signature and date

Your offer letter needn't necessarily include all of the items shown above. It could be that Human Resources has strict control over the form your offer letter will take. However, an offer letter should include title, salary, and an overview of benefits.

Some offer letters are constructed to limit an organization's liability (*e.g., they may include a clause about the termination of employment by either party*). You need to seek professional input on this subject from a Human Resources representative or a lawyer.

No matter how limited or extensive your offer letter, be sure to read it exactly as written when making your verbal offer. Refrain from any *"off-the-cuff"* comments at this time. You are extending a verbal contract.

It is, however, perfectly appropriate for you to congratulate the candidate. Chances are he will be very pleased to hear that he has been selected. Just don't go overboard and say something like, *"When you sign on at Firm ABC, we'll take care of you for life!"* Comments like this can create problems later.

Sometimes, your offer may be rejected. The candidate may have gotten a better offer, or decided to look for a different position. Refusals aren't uncommon—they take place approximately 20 percent of the time. In fact, if your offers are always accepted, you may want to take a hard look at the salaries you are offering. A 100 percent acceptance rate is a possible indicator that the salaries you're offering are too high!

At times, your initial offer may need to be adjusted. After reading the offer letter to your final candidate, ask for any comments or questions. You may be able to handle minor adjustments on the spot. If you need to make significant changes to either the salary or benefits, however, contact Human Resources or another internal expert within your organization to make sure that the request is acceptable.

Whatever the case, you may need to update your offer letter to reflect any changes before sending it to the candidate. Send two copies of the final letter as soon as possible. The candidate keeps one for personal records, and your organization retains the returned, signed copy.

Back at Mother Earth, Inc.,...

Anika went ahead and checked references on all three of her top candidates, starting with Lizbeth. She figured the practice would do her good and she could get comfortable with the process before checking on Eric, her top candidate.

The reference checks revealed no new information. The people Anika contacted were mostly supportive, and one actually raved about Cheryl's technical expertise.

This done, Anika worked with Human Resources to put together the offer letter for Eric. The Human Resources professional she consulted looked at the salaries of other employees at Mother Earth with job titles and responsibilities similar to the open position. This ensured that the offer was internally fair as well as externally competitive. Since the pay structure at Mother Earth outranked most in the market, Anika felt confident that Eric would be thrilled with the offer. Smiling to herself, she closed the door to Greg Chandler's office, sat down, and dialed the phone.

"*This is Eric. May I help you?*" Eric said as he picked up the phone.

"*Eric, this is Anika Jordan from Mother Earth. Is now a good time to talk?*" Anika asked.

Eric responded affirmatively, so Anika went over the details of the offer letter. Eric listened politely until she was finished, then cleared his throat. There was a long pause.

"*Eric, are you still there?*" Anika asked.

"*Yes, but, well, I have some news,*" Eric replied, then rapidly continued. "*Somehow, someone in my department figured out that I was going on interviews and leaked it to my supervisor. We had a meeting, and it turns out that she is willing to do what it takes to keep me on board here. When I told her about wanting to finish my master's degree, she agreed to help with that, too. While the salary you've offered is definitely attractive, the package they've put together for me here is even better, and I won't have to go through the hassle of changing jobs!*"

Anika was surprised by the mix of exasperation, disappointment, and surprise that she felt upon hearing this news. Outwardly, she took it philosophically. "*I'm very happy to hear that things are going to work out for you, Eric. I wish you every success,*" Anika responded. "*And if things don't work out, please give me a call, so we can talk about any opportunities that might exist at Mother Earth,*" she added.

"*Thanks! I hope I haven't caused you any trouble,*" Eric replied before hanging up.

> Anika leaned back in her chair and sighed. Colleagues had warned her that the selection process could be somewhat tiresome. Now, she believed it. She gathered up her offer letter and headed back to Human Resources, where she began to formulate an offer letter for Cheryl, the next candidate in line.
>
> Things went more smoothly when Anika offered the receptionist position to Cheryl, who seemed very pleased with the terms of the offer. Cheryl would soon be on board at Mother Earth. Despite Eric's refusal, Anika felt pleased with herself and her experience using the Performance-Based Selection Process....

If you receive a positive response to your verbal offer, immediately send out the offer letter *(try to use an overnight service)*, so that you can get the signed letter back as soon as possible. At this point, you should feel confident that you have done all that you possibly can to make sure that the person you hired will fit well within your organization. However, you also need to start thinking about the orientation process for your new hire *(for some ideas, see the guidebook, On-The-Job Orientation And Training, published by Richard Chang Associates, Inc.).*

Go ahead and congratulate yourself for orchestrating a successful hire, but don't forget that there's one more task yet to perform. You need to tie up some loose ends.

Inform Non-Selected Candidates Of Your Decision

Each and every applicant for the open position deserves either a written or a verbal rejection. This may sound unrealistic, especially if you have received one hundred or more resumes, but it's really not as big a task as it seems.

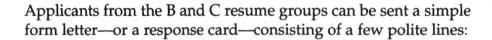

Applicants from the B and C resume groups can be sent a simple form letter—or a response card—consisting of a few polite lines:

Dear_____:

Thank you for your interest in Mother Earth, Inc. While we do not see a fit between your background and the open position at this time, we will keep your resume on file and contact you if a suitable position becomes available.

Once again, thank you for your interest in Mother Earth, Inc.

When composing your letter, make sure to include a line *(such as "keeping your resume on file")* that will keep applicants interested in your organization. In addition, it is often a good idea to put in a line that emphasizes the applicant's strengths *(e.g., "While your credentials are impressive...")*. Remember that the rejected applicant may actually fit your needs as a candidate in the future, or may be or become a customer of or a supplier to your organization. Word your letter in a way that reflects positively on your organization's image.

The letter should be signed by the supervisor of the position or a Human Resources representative. Likewise, applicants who were screened by phone should be sent a similar letter, signed by the person who conducted the phone screen.

Handle verbal rejections in an equally diplomatic manner. Any candidate with whom you met face-to-face should be informed of your decision over the phone. While many supervisors try to skip this courtesy, it reflects better on you and your organization if you inform the candidate personally over the phone.

It needn't be a big deal. Just call your candidates, ask if they have time for a brief conversation, and then immediately tell them the reason for your call. Don't think that easing into the subject by working up to it slowly will make them more comfortable; in all likelihood, they've already guessed that you've called either to make an offer or to reject them.

Simply tell the non-selected candidates that you've found another candidate who is a better fit for the position. Thank them for coming in for an interview. If you foresee a possible fit in the future, it is appropriate to say so. Avoid raising false hopes, however.

Also keep from relating a specific reason for the rejection. You may not really have one; besides, if you do, you don't want to be put in the position of defending your choice. At this point, the rejected candidate may be feeling anything from disappointment to anger or hurt. Don't provide an opportunity to begin an argument with you.

At Mother Earth, Inc.,...

Anika burst into Pat's office. *"Well, I did it. We have a new receptionist,"* Anika told her.

"Good job!" Pat replied. *"But aren't you forgetting something?"* she asked.

"Nope. If you're referring to the rejection letters, I had Carl run a mail merge this morning, and I'm on my way to call the others as we speak," Anika responded.

"Well, aren't you efficient!" Pat laughed.

"Hey, you have to be, when you're the Marketing Coordinator for Mother Earth, Incorporated!" Anika quipped.

Congratulations! You've got your high-performing candidate on board. Don't just sit back and wait for results, however. Even a new employee with the best possible qualifications and expertise won't operate at peak performance without proper orientation, training, guidance, and evaluation. Listed at the end of this guidebook are other titles that can help you bring out the best in your employees.

CHAPTER SEVEN WORKSHEET: PUTTING TOGETHER YOUR OFFER

1. Ask Human Resources for a blank template of your organization's offer letter, or take a look at your own. Would you change the letter, keep it the same, or start from scratch? List any of your ideas for changes here. *(Note: If you intend to use the new letter you have created, be sure to run it past Human Resources before you submit it to a candidate.)*

_____

_____

_____

_____

_____

_____

_____

_____

_____

_____

_____

_____

_____

_____

2. In what ways would you be willing to adjust your offer if your candidate requests it? What components of an offer are *"negotiable"*? Which are *"non-negotiable"*?

_____

_____

_____

_____

_____

_____

_____

_____

_____

_____

_____

_____

_____

_____

_____

_____

_____

_____

_____

3. You are about to make a call to inform a non-selected candidate of your decision. What will you say? How will you answer the question, *"Why was I not selected..."*?

_____

_____

_____

_____

_____

_____

_____

_____

_____

_____

_____

_____

_____

_____

_____

_____

_____

_____

CHAPTER EIGHT

SUMMARY

The Performance-Based Selection Process you have learned about in this guidebook was created from real-world experience and proven methodology. Its basic principle, that of basing your hiring decisions on past performance and behaviors, will result not only in selecting candidates who are the best fit for your organization, but also in selecting candidates who will be more likely to stay with your organization on a long-term basis.

Remember, most employees leave a position due to poor on-the-job behavior, not lack of technical skills. Finding a candidate who is the perfect mix of attitude and aptitude can be tough. If you go about the selection process haphazardly, you'll never be able to track how you happened to get successful candidates on board.

If you apply the same process consistently, you increase your chances of making successful hires on a regular basis. The Performance-Based Selection Process will help you do this.

Read each chapter of this guidebook carefully. Put some thought and effort into the worksheets. Study the forms and sheets contained in the Appendix and think about how you are going to use them.

Also, enlist help from your colleagues or others in your organization. Their assistance will be instrumental in determining the requirements of the open position, the designing of performance-based questions, the conducting of applicant screening, the interviewing of candidates, and especially in the selecting of your final candidate.

It is said that people make their own luck. People who appear lucky really have put thought and effort into considering their choices, both in the workplace and in their personal lives. Do something to make yourself that *"lucky"* person who brings all the best people into your organization. Use *Interviewing And Selecting High Performers* the next time you have to hire someone. You won't regret it!

REPRODUCIBLE FORMS AND WORKSHEETS

Reference Material

Reproducible Forms

The pages in the Appendix are provided for you to photocopy and use appropriately.

RECRUITING CHECKLIST
REQUIREMENTS

What You Need To Do/Have Prior To Recruiting

☐ Staffing Need

☐ Current Job Description/ Position Requirements Worksheet

☐ Employment Requisition

☐ Company Authorization

☐ Budget Considerations

☐ Know Your Organization's Business Plans, and Policies and Procedures

☐ Input From Past Incumbent, and Past Management Team Members

☐ Performance-Based Interview Questions

☐ Legal Guidelines/Compliance

RESOURCES

Where You And Others In Your Organization May Find Applicants

☐ Current Employees

☐ Current Temp Employees and Contractors

☐ Employee Referrals

☐ Networking

☐ Data Base/Mailing Lists

☐ Newly Arrived Applications/ Resumes

☐ *"Walk-ins"*

☐ *"Declined Offer"* Files

☐ Professional Associations

☐ Past Voluntary Terminations/ Layoffs

☐ Colleges and Universities

☐ Other Companies' Organizational Charts

☐ Other Companies' Layoffs

☐ Press Releases of Other Companies' Reorganizations

☐ Temporary Agencies

☐ Advertising Agencies

METHODS

How You And Others In Your Organization May Inform Applicants Of Your Open Position

☐ Communications from/ with Human Resources Staff

☐ Employee and Vendor Referrals

☐ Bulletins

☐ Employee Publications

☐ Direct Mailings/Memos

☐ *"Open Houses"*

☐ Job Fairs

☐ College Placement Centers

☐ Professional/Trade Associations' Newsletters

☐ Announcements at Professional Gatherings

☐ Direct/Indirect Solicitations

☐ Media Advertising–Newspapers and Magazines

☐ Professional Employment Agencies

☐ *"Word of Mouth"*

☐ Job Posting Program

WHAT'S A GOOD QUESTION?
*(The Do's And Don'ts Of Creating Worthwhile
Performance-Based Questions)*

☆ Do ask for contrasts and comparisons.
Example: *"Please compare your duties at your last organization with those at another company where you held the same position."*

☆ Do ask for clarification of *"jargon."*
Example: *"Please explain what you mean by 'pull marketing.'"*

☆ Do use plural rather than singular nouns.
Example: *"Describe the <u>times</u> when you felt best about your career."*

☆ Don't test assumptions by offering guesses about facts.
Example: *"I suppose you would have been 'fed up' by then and quit, right?"*

☆ Don't collect information not relevant to the behaviors you are looking for.
Example: *"Have you seen Elvis lately?"*

☆ Don't ask questions that are an invasion of privacy.
Example: *"Tell me how you 'selected' your wife."*

☆ Don't ask multiple-choice questions.
Example: *"Then did you go to your boss, tell the customer off, or keep quiet?"*

☆ Don't express value judgments in your questions.
Example: *"How did you get involved in such a worthless operation?"*

☆ Don't make the interview appear to be an interrogation.
Example: *"You really don't know why?"*

PERFORMANCE-BASED INTERVIEW QUESTIONS
(Sorted By Demonstrated Behavior Or Trait)

Responsibility

1. For what tasks in your previous position did you have full responsibility?

2. Describe a time when you were criticized for the way you handled a project.

3. What are some of the problems you have encountered while performing in your current position, and how did you handle them?

4. How do you manage to meet your responsibilities in your absence *(e.g., planned vacations, off-site commitments, or unplanned illness, etc.)*?

Organization

1. How do you organize your work day?

2. What is your procedure for meeting deadlines?

3. What have you done when you've found yourself swamped?

4. What timesaving ideas work for you? How did you discover them?

Communication Skills

1. What makes you effective when you are speaking before a group of people?

2. What have you found to be the most effective way of communicating an idea, and persuading peers to your point of view? Your manager?

3. What difficulties have you encountered which were caused by poor communication on your part, or on the part of others?

Enthusiasm For Customer Service

1. How do you define customer service? How do you define quality?

2. What types of customer-service improvement programs were you part of in your last position?

3. Describe the kinds of quality improvements you were part of in your last position. What were your responsibilities and contributions?

4. What worked and did not work in your customer-service improvement efforts at your last position?

Interpersonal Relations

1. How did you establish your relationship with your past manager? Describe how it has led to a good or poor working relationship.

2. How did your past manager evaluate your job performance? If there were discrepancies, how did you resolve them?

3. What kind of people do you like to work with? What type do you find most difficult to work with?

4. What have you done in the past when you've had to work closely with someone with whom you've disagreed, or had a conflict?

5. What have you done when someone has voiced opinions that differ from yours, especially about something you feel strongly about?

6. Tell me about a typical customer-service problem at your last organization. How did you handle it?

7. If you could create the ideal department and people you would like to work for and with, what would it be like?

Leadership

1. What techniques have you used in your work to get others—either managers, colleagues, or employees who report to you—enthusiastic about your projects?

2. How have you delegated responsibility to others?

3. How do you meet your deadlines when people who don't report to you are called upon to support your work?

4. What motivates you to do a good job?

Teamwork

1. Describe a project you worked on as a member of a team in your last job.

    What was your contribution?
    What would you do to make that team or project more successful today?
2. What are your particular strengths as a team member?

3. What are your particular weaknesses as a team member?

4. What would your teammates say about you?

Career Interests

1. What is your overall career objective? What have you done or plan to do to assist yourself in reaching this objective?

2. What do you feel has contributed *most* to the successes *(or failures)* you've experienced in your career?

3. What are you looking for in this job that you *didn't* find in your past job?

4. How do you feel about the progress you have made with your present/last organization, and why?

5. Do you consider your progress on your last job representative of your ability, and why?

6. What are some of the things in a job that are important to you, and why?

7. What are some of the things you would like to avoid in a job, and why?

8. What are some of the things that motivate you in a job?

9. What disappointments *(e.g., failures, challenges, etc.)* have you found beneficial in your development? Why?

Flexibility

1. Tell me about a time when your routine was disrupted. How did you handle it?

2. How have you responded when you encountered unforeseen obstacles in a project you were working on?

3. What have you done when others *(e.g., your manager, supervisor, etc.)* have resisted your ideas/recommendations?

4. How do you deal with situations in which you do not fare favorably?

Initiative

1. How have your responsibilities changed since you started your present job?

2. What new procedures or improvements did you bring to your last job?

3. What goals have you set for yourself which you've achieved?

4. If you were chosen for this job, how would you want us to assist you in your work?

Judgment

1. Tell me about a time when you were confronted by a problem that seemed to demand your manager's attention, and he/she was not available.

2. How do you decide on whom to ask for advice?

3. Why have you decided to leave your present job? *(Always seek more than one reason for a voluntary resignation.)*

4. Why are you interested in *this* position?

5. What would you say was the most, or least interesting job you ever had, and what are your reasons for feeling this way?

6. Where would you rank your last job with other jobs you have held, and why?

7. What would you change in your current/last working environment?

Detail Orientation

1. What did you do when your work was returned to you for correction?

2. How did you maintain accuracy during periods of frequent interruptions?

3. What aspects of your previous job demanded specific attention to detail?

Quality

1. How did your last organization define quality?

2. What types of customer-service improvement programs were you part of in your last position?

3. Describe the kinds of quality improvements you were part of in your last job. What were your responsibilities and contributions?

4. What worked and what did not work in your quality-improvement efforts on your last job?

POSITION REQUIREMENTS WORKSHEET

Title: **Date Open:**
Need For Position:

FUNCTIONS AND RESPONSIBILITIES

I.   III.

  A.   A.

  B.   B.

  C.   C.

I.   IV.

  A.   A.

  B.   B.

  C.   C.

TECHNICAL SKILLS	OTHER REQUIREMENTS

PERFORMANCE-BASED INTERVIEW QUESTIONS WORKSHEET

OPEN POSITION:		
FUNCTIONS AND RESPONSIBLITIES	**DEMONSTRATED BEHAVIORS OR TRAITS**	**PERFORMANCE-BASED INTERVIEW QUESTIONS**
I.		
A.	1.	1. 2.
B.	2.	3. 4.
C.	3.	5. 6.
II.		
A.	1.	7. 8.
B.	2.	9. 10.
C.	3.	11. 12.
III.		
A.	1.	13. 14.
B.	2.	15. 16.
C.	3.	17. 18.

PHONE SCREEN ORGANIZER

CANDIDATE NAME:	DATE/TIME:
RESUME-RELATED QUESTIONS *(e.g., employment status, current pay, location, etc.)*	**RESPONSES**
1.	1.
2.	2.
3.	3.
4.	4.
5.	5.
JOB-RELATED QUESTIONS *(e.g., travel, salary requirements, work environment, etc.)*	**RESPONSES**
1.	1.
2.	2.
3.	3.
4.	4.
5.	5.

INTERVIEW NOTES		
Name of Interviewer:	**Date:**	
Name of Candidate:	**Position:**	

QUESTION #:	RESPONSE TO QUESTIONS	RATING (1-5) 1 = Not a fit 5 = Excellent fit

ADDITIONAL COMMENTS:

Final recommendation: ☐ Hire ☐ Don't Hire

RATIONALE:

CANDIDATE COMPARISON SHEET

N: Name C: Last Company/Position S: Last Annual Salary O: Other Compensation Y: Years Of Direct Experience	Candidate #1 N: C: S: O: Y:	Candidate #2 N: C: S: O: Y:	Candidate #3 N: C: S: O: Y:
Test Score			
Test Score			
Overall Rating—Question # 1			
Overall Rating—Question # 2			
Overall Rating—Question # 3			
Overall Rating—Question # 4			
Overall Rating—Question # 5			
Overall Rating—Question # 6			
(Other):			
Overall Interview Rating			
Rank Order			

Professional And Personal Development Publications From Richard Chang Associates, Inc.

Designed to support continuous learning, these highly targeted, integrated collections from Richard Chang Associates, Inc. (RCA) help individuals and organizations acquire the knowledge and skills needed to succeed in today's ever-changing workplace. Titles are available through RCA, Jossey-Bass, Inc., fine bookstores, and distributors internationally.

Practical Guidebook Collection

Quality Improvement Series
Continuous Process Improvement
Continuous Improvement Tools, Volume 1
Continuous Improvement Tools, Volume 2
Step-By-Step Problem Solving
Meetings That Work!
Improving Through Benchmarking
Succeeding As A Self-Managed Team
Measuring Organizational Improvement Impact
Process Reengineering In Action
Satisfying Internal Customers First!

Management Skills Series
Interviewing And Selecting High Performers
On-The-Job Orientation And Training
Coaching Through Effective Feedback
Expanding Leadership Impact
Mastering Change Management
Re-Creating Teams During Transitions
Planning Successful Employee Performance
Coaching For Peak Employee Performance
Evaluating Employee Performance

High Performance Team Series
Success Through Teamwork
Building A Dynamic Team
Measuring Team Performance
Team Decision-Making Techniques

High-Impact Training Series
Creating High-Impact Training
Identifying Targeted Training Needs
Mapping A Winning Training Approach
Producing High-Impact Learning Tools
Applying Successful Training Techniques
Measuring The Impact Of Training
Make Your Training Results Last

Workplace Diversity Series
Capitalizing On Workplace Diversity
Successful Staffing In A Diverse Workplace
Team Building For Diverse Work Groups
Communicating In A Diverse Workplace
Tools For Valuing Diversity

Personal Growth And Development Collection

Managing Your Career in a Changing Workplace
Unlocking Your Career Potential
Marketing Yourself and Your Career
Making Career Transitions
Memory Tips For The Forgetful

101 Stupid Things Collection

101 Stupid Things Trainers Do To Sabotage Success
101 Stupid Things Supervisors Do To Sabotage Success
101 Stupid Things Employees Do To Sabotage Success
101 Stupid Things Salespeople Do To Sabotage Success
101 Stupid Things Business Travelers Do To Sabotage Success

About Richard Chang Associates, Inc.

Richard Chang Associates, Inc. (RCA) is a multi-disciplinary organizational performance improvement firm. Since 1987, RCA has provided private and public sector clients around the world with the experience, expertise, and resources needed to build capability in such critical areas as process improvement, management development, project management, team performance, performance measurement, and facilitator training. RCA's comprehensive package of services, products, and publications reflect the firm's commitment to practical, innovative approaches and to the achievement of significant, measurable results.

RCA Resources Optimize Organizational Performance

Consulting — Using a broad range of skills, knowledge, and tools, RCA consultants assist clients in developing and implementing a wide range of performance improvement initiatives.

Training — Practical, "real world" training programs are designed with a "take initiative" emphasis. Options include off-the-shelf programs, customized programs, and public and on-site seminars.

Curriculum And Materials Development — A cost-effective and flexible alternative to internal staffing, RCA can custom-develop and/or customize content to meet both organizational objectives and specific program needs.

Video Production — RCA's award-winning, custom video productions provide employees with information in a consistent manner that achieves lasting impact.

Publications — The comprehensive and practical collection of publications from RCA supports organizational training initiatives and self-directed learning.

Packaged Programs — Designed for first-time and experienced trainers alike, these programs offer comprehensive, integrated materials (including selected Practical Guidebooks) that provide a wide range of flexible training options. Choose from:

- Meetings That Work! ToolPAK™
- Step-By-Step Problem Solving ToolKIT™
- Continuous Process Improvement Packaged Training Program
- Continuous Improvement Tools, Volume 1 ToolPAK™
- Continuous Improvement Tools, Volume 2 ToolPAK™
- High Involvement Teamwork™ Packaged Training Program

RICHARD
CHANG
ASSOCIATES

World Class Resources. World Class Results.℠

Richard Chang Associates, Inc.
Corporate Headquarters
15265 Alton Parkway, Suite 300, Irvine, California 92618 USA
(800) 756-8096 • (949) 727-7477 • Fax: (949) 727-7007
E-Mail: info@rca4results.com • www.richardchangassociates.com

U.S. Offices in Irvine and Atlanta • Licensees and Distributors Worldwide